# OFFICIAL
# FORTNITE
## SUPPLY DROP
### COLLECTORS' EDITION

ⓁⒷ

# CONTENTS

THIS IS YOUR ULTIMATE GUIDE TO WEAPONS
IN FORTNITE. GEAR UP AND GET READY FOR A BATTLE ROYALE!

# FEATURES

# WEAPONS

# SUPPLY DROP INCOMING!

## CRACK OPEN A CRATE OF GREAT GUNS, INSANE ITEMS, AND AWESOME ADVICE WITH THIS HANDBOOK

Fortnite's supply drops are always loaded with goodies. As soon as you see that crate floating down to the island, you want to drop everything and make a run for it. You have no way of telling what you'll find inside, but that's half the fun. True to the spirit of those beautiful boxes of booty, we've loaded up this book with all of the best gear in the game—hopefully it will help you on your way to Victory Royale.

In Fortnite, there's no such thing as a bad weapon. In the right hands, even a lowly Common gun can rack up plenty of eliminations, while the rarest and most powerful weapons make that process a little easier for everyone.

The arsenal of Fortnite changes all the time, with older items sent to the Vault to make room for new arrivals, keeping the action fresh and interesting for each new season. With the landscape of the game constantly shifting like this, we've done all we can to make sure the contents of this book are as accurate as possible up to and including Season 9, although weapons stats and availability can change overnight—you might find you need to wait a while to try out some of these wonderful toys, but they may come back eventually.

## KNOWLEDGE IS POWER!

## USE THE ENVIRONMENT TO YOUR ADVANTAGE

Foliage provides natural cover, but you'll still need to keep low and move slowly to avoid detection. Where possible, it's always best to have the high ground advantage when engaging enemies, and being up high can also sometimes put you out of the ground-level sightlines of opponents. Again, avoid unnecessary movement so as not to give yourself away.

# LEGENDARY LOOT

## WHAT FORTNITE'S ITEM RARITY SYSTEM MEANS TO YOU

Not all weapons are created equal. In the world of Fortnite, the color-coded rarity scale is a measure of an item's power and an indication of how likely you are to come across one on the island. Rocket Launchers only come in the top tiers, and are therefore quite scarce, while weapons that have Common and Uncommon variants are what you're likely to stumble upon first. Even a Common Assault Rifle can be a monster, but more powerful versions can make a Victory Royale easier. Never assume that rarer weapons spell instant victory, though. Smart building, pinpoint accuracy, and sneaky movement can all help to turn the tables.

# GUNNING FOR GEAR
## IT'S NOT JUST WEAPONS THAT HAVE RARITY TIERS

You're probably used to Fortnite's color-coded rarity tiers. If not, it's time to learn your Uncommons from your Epics, as the system is used throughout the game. Every item in the game is assigned a tier, and this gives you an idea of how scarce each is.

# COMMON

The lowest of the five rarity tiers in Fortnite, Common weapons can be found just about everywhere. They're perfect for plugging any holes in your arsenal until something better shows up. They might not seem like much, but they can be lifesavers.

## UNCOMMON

These will often be your go-to tools for the first encounter or two. The stats are typically only marginally better than Common weapons, so both are well suited to the early game when a lot of opposing players won't have buffed themselves with shields. These are basic weapons, but they'll serve you well.

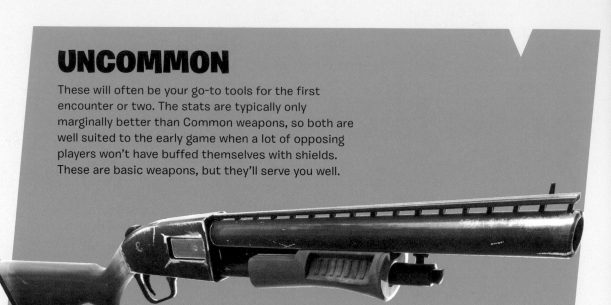

## RARE

As you move up through the tiers, the chances of finding special weapons get slimmer. Instead, you need to be looting chests, so fire up Playground Mode and explore all the different places these can spawn. In actual games, only some of these spots will spawn, so knowing likely locations will help your chances.

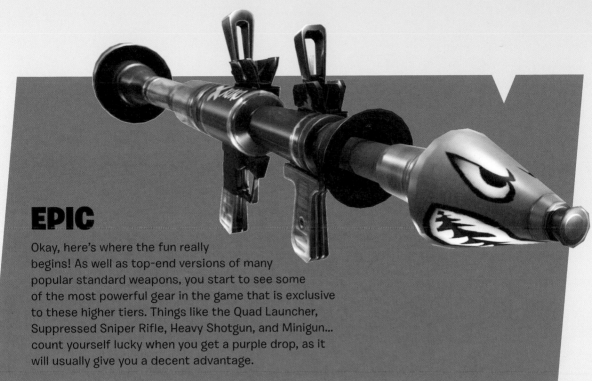

# EPIC

Okay, here's where the fun really begins! As well as top-end versions of many popular standard weapons, you start to see some of the most powerful gear in the game that is exclusive to these higher tiers. Things like the Quad Launcher, Suppressed Sniper Rifle, Heavy Shotgun, and Minigun... count yourself lucky when you get a purple drop, as it will usually give you a decent advantage.

# LEGENDARY

The best of the best, but also the rarest. You can rest easy knowing that you'll be difficult to outgun if you have one of these, but remember that if you're not making your shots count, you can still be downed by players with better aim!

## KNOWLEDGE IS POWER!

## RETREAT IS NOT A COWARDLY OPTION

It's one thing to have the guts to go toe-to-toe with anyone you run into, but quite another to know when the odds aren't in your favor. There's no shame in laying low or turning tail if it's clear you're heading into trouble—letting other players deal with one another is a tried and true way of getting into the last few survivors!

# GUNNING FOR GLORY

**ASSAULT RIFLES ARE WELL-ROUNDED, THOUGH NOT FLASHY, AND EFFECTIVE AT JUST ABOUT ANY RANGE**

Assault Rifles come in several shapes and sizes, and fit a variety of needs within the Fortnite universe. The basic Assault Rifle, in all of its variations, is an acceptable tool for just about anything you need to accomplish, with its well-rounded stats, decent damage and ammo capacity, good accuracy, and even a snappy rate of fire.

As long as you're not trying to unload an entire clip at once and you remember to fire in short bursts, you'll be golden, whether you're trying to make a quick getaway or rack up some wins on your way to a Victory Royale. It's a gun that, no matter what kind of situation you're in, you're never disappointed to find.

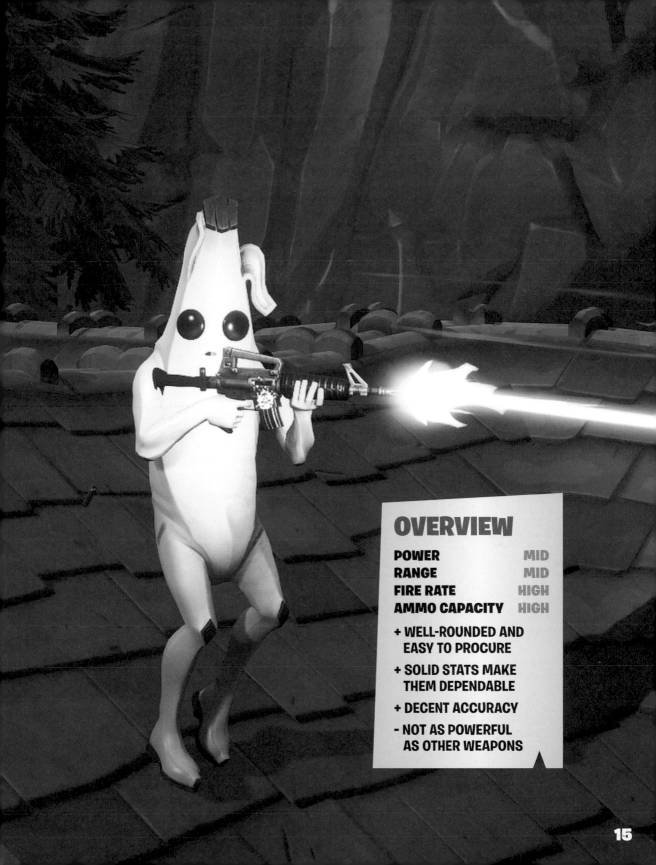

## OVERVIEW

| | |
|---|---|
| **POWER** | MID |
| **RANGE** | MID |
| **FIRE RATE** | HIGH |
| **AMMO CAPACITY** | HIGH |

+ WELL-ROUNDED AND EASY TO PROCURE

+ SOLID STATS MAKE THEM DEPENDABLE

+ DECENT ACCURACY

- NOT AS POWERFUL AS OTHER WEAPONS

# ASSAULT RIFLE

## COMMON
### ASSAULT RIFLE

**DAMAGE:** LOW **FIRE RATE:** HIGH
**AMMO CAPACITY:** HIGH **RELOAD TIME:** LOW

**A STALWART FAVORITE THAT'S EASY TO FIND**

This flexible rifle is a basic, no-nonsense weapon capable of handling just about any type of situation. Thanks to flinging nearly six bullets per second at targets, it's a decent start on your road to victory.

**TIP**
To increase shot accuracy, you can opt to stand or crouch, then aim down the sights.

## UNCOMMON
### ASSAULT RIFLE

**DAMAGE:** LOW **FIRE RATE:** HIGH
**AMMO CAPACITY:** HIGH **RELOAD TIME:** LOW

**KICK THINGS UP A NOTCH**

Sometimes, you need a little more firepower, and that's where the Uncommon Assault Rifle comes in. It ups the damage slightly and reduces reload time to pack a meatier punch, and you should be pleased to find this one.

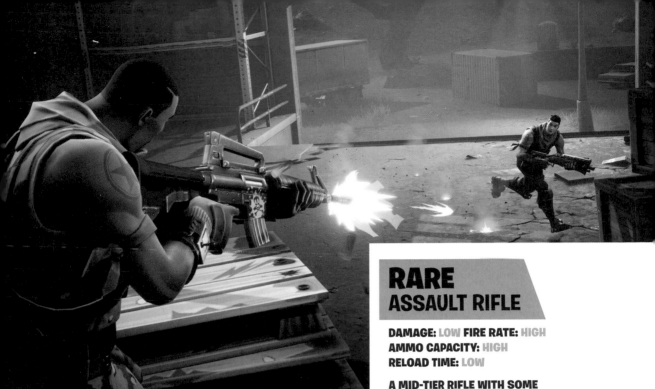

## RARE
### ASSAULT RIFLE

**DAMAGE:** LOW **FIRE RATE:** HIGH
**AMMO CAPACITY:** HIGH
**RELOAD TIME:** LOW

#### A MID-TIER RIFLE WITH SOME SERIOUS PUNCH

A pretty significant upgrade over the Uncommon version. Never underestimate how strong a standard machine gun can be!

## EPIC
### ASSAULT RIFLE

**DAMAGE:** MID **FIRE RATE:** HIGH
**AMMO CAPACITY:** HIGH
**RELOAD TIME:** LOW

#### A POWERFUL EVOLUTION OF A CLASSIC

The Epic Assault Rifle makes a big leap from the first three tiers of Assault Rifles. Like the Legendary version, it looks quite a bit different from its fast-firing brethren, and you'll start to recognize them when you see them.

# LEGENDARY
## ASSAULT RIFLE

**DAMAGE:** MID **FIRE RATE** HIGH
**AMMO CAPACITY:** HIGH **RELOAD TIME:** LOW

### THE BEST ASSAULT RIFLE YOU'LL FIND IN FORTNITE

The Legendary variant of the Assault Rifle is one of the best you can hope to stumble upon. It takes the already-impressive damage, fire rate, and reload speed, and bolsters them big time. If you're looking for some serious firepower, grab one of these and don't let go.

# BURST ASSAULT RIFLE

## COMMON
### BURST ASSAULT RIFLE

**DAMAGE:** LOW **FIRE RATE:** MID
**AMMO CAPACITY:** HIGH **RELOAD TIME:** MID

## AN ACCURATE TWIST ON
## THE AUTOMATIC RIFLE

The Burst Assault Rifle is a versatile weapon great for any situation. However, it does have a lower fire rate than the other Assault Rifles in the game, and you won't be able to continue unloading an entire mag into an enemy, since it fires in bursts as its name implies.

# UNCOMMON
## BURST ASSAULT RIFLE

**DAMAGE:** LOW **FIRE RATE:** MID
**AMMO CAPACITY:** HIGH **RELOAD TIME:** MID

### A SLIGHT UPGRADE WITH A THREE-ROUND BURST THAT REALLY STINGS

This Uncommon version raises all stats slightly, upping overall damage. Its low fire rate necessitates the three-round burst, so it's best used with caution and accuracy rather than as a spray-and-pray weapon.

## FACT
The Common, Uncommon, and Rare Burst Assault Rifles use the same model as Save the World's Semi-Auto Rifle.

## FACT

Fans often refer to the Burst Assault Rifle as the "Burst," "Triple Burst," and various other names.

# RARE
## BURST ASSAULT RIFLE

**DAMAGE:** LOW **FIRE RATE:** MID
**AMMO CAPACITY:** HIGH **RELOAD TIME:** MID

### A RELIABLE AND ACCURATE CHOICE FOR BOLSTERED ASSAULT RIFLE FANS

This slightly more powerful Rare twist on the Burst Assault Rifle continues to improve its accuracy. You can also enhance it farther by ensuring you keep the correct amount of distance between yourself and your enemies. Don't be afraid to close in on opponents when they attempt to get away!

# EPIC
## BURST ASSAULT RIFLE

**DAMAGE:** LOW **FIRE RATE:** MID
**AMMO CAPACITY:** HIGH
**RELOAD TIME:** MID

### AN ACCURATE RIFF ON THE ASSAULT RIFLE THAT'S A LITTLE HARDER TO FIND

This midrange Burst Assault Rifle is a little more difficult to procure, but it also continues the natural progression in-game by improving in all areas in terms of stats. If you can find one then you don't really need to go the extra mile and keep gunning for a Legendary variant, as this Epic version will do you just fine for the remainder of the game, and ammo should still be quite plentiful.

FACT
You may need to aim a little lower than usual to adjust for this weapon's recoil.

## TIP
Try crouching while aiming the rifle at your opponents to increase the accuracy of your first few shots.

# LEGENDARY
## BURST ASSAULT RIFLE

**DAMAGE:** LOW **FIRE RATE:** MID
**AMMO CAPACITY:** HIGH **RELOAD TIME:** LOW

### THE DEFINITIVE BURST ASSAULT RIFLE, AS DANGEROUS AS THEY COME

The Legendary Burst Assault Rifle is no lightweight, though the fire rate isn't as high as you'd expect from a typical Assault Rifle. However, at medium range, it truly shines, and it puts the accuracy of the other Assault Rifles in the game to shame.

## RARE
## SCOPED ASSAULT RIFLE

**DAMAGE:** LOW **FIRE RATE:** MID
**AMMO CAPACITY:** MID **RELOAD TIME:** MID

### AN ASSAULT RIFLE WITH THE
### HEART OF A SNIPER

You'll likely become a better sniper as you use this hybrid rifle, so it's worth considering if you're trying to develop a more rounded skill set. It may be incapable of sending a torrent of shots hurtling toward an enemy, but it will force you to slow down and think carefully about where you're aiming.

## FACT
The Scoped Assault Rifle has 100% accuracy when the scope is used.

## TIP

Don't carry only a Scoped Assault Rifle just in case you're met with medium-range enemies.

## EPIC
### SCOPED ASSAULT RIFLE

**DAMAGE:** LOW **FIRE RATE:** MID
**AMMO CAPACITY:** MID **RELOAD TIME:** LOW

**PRACTICE YOUR SNIPING SKILLS WITH THIS RIDICULOUSLY POWERFUL RIFLE**

The Scoped Assault Rifle is worth keeping around in your inventory even if you happen upon a different, more powerful weapon. You can keep it alongside a regular Assault Rifle to have a 100% accurate long-range weapon handy as well as a medium-range weapon to swap between, just in case.

# HEAVY ASSAULT RIFLE

## COMMON
### HEAVY ASSAULT RIFLE

**DAMAGE:** MID **FIRE RATE:** MID
**AMMO CAPACITY:** MID **RELOAD TIME:** MID

**SPRAY AND PRAY WITH CONFIDENCE WITH THIS POWERFUL ASSAULT RIFLE OPTION**

While the Assault Rifle is appropriate for a variety of situations, the Heavy Assault Rifle is better suited to clearing out loads of enemies. It has high damage, reliable kick when the trigger is held, and great headshot potential. You trade all this for a slower fire rate, but when it's this powerful, it hardly matters.

## FACT
The Heavy Assault Rifle first made its in-game appearance with Update 6.22.

# UNCOMMON
## HEAVY ASSAULT RIFLE

**DAMAGE:** MID **FIRE RATE:** MID
**AMMO CAPACITY:** MID **RELOAD TIME:** MID

### A FORMIDABLE ASSAULT RIFLE WITH A CONSIDERABLE KICK

This slightly more powerful Heavy Assault Rifle ups the ante in terms of damage. While it can overtake just about any opponent who won't know what hit them, you won't want to hold down the trigger too long, as its accuracy will very quickly fall off.

## TIP
The Heavy Assault Rifle's accuracy isn't the best, so take your time to aim your shots carefully.

## RARE
### HEAVY ASSAULT RIFLE

**DAMAGE:** MID **FIRE RATE:** MID
**AMMO CAPACITY:** MID **RELOAD TIME:** MID

**AN UNSTOPPABLE RIFLE THAT CAN
BLOW AWAY THE COMPETITION**

The most souped-up version of the Heavy Assault Rifle is a must-have in your arsenal. Even without an enormous magazine, it's still more than capable of destroying anyone who dares cross you. Swap out your Heavy Assault Rifle with a regular Assault Rifle if you need a peppier spray of bullets, and you won't go too far wrong.

# MINIGUN

## EPIC
### MINIGUN

**DAMAGE:** LOW **FIRE RATE:** HIGH
**AMMO CAPACITY:** HIGH
**RELOAD TIME:** N/A

### SERIOUS FIREPOWER THAT TAKES TIME TO SPIN UP

The Minigun is an absolutely devastating gun that's über powerful. If you're unlucky enough to get in its path, you'll want to seriously rethink that decision. It can take a while to get started spewing bullets, but once it's cranked up and ready, it can spray torrents of metal until it runs out of ammo or overheats.

## LEGENDARY
### MINIGUN

**DAMAGE:** LOW **FIRE RATE:** HIGH
**AMMO CAPACITY:** HIGH
**RELOAD TIME:** N/A

### A SLOW STARTER WITH A HIGH RATE OF FIRE

The best version of the Minigun. Plant yourself in a defensive position and lay down a constant stream of bullets. Then sit back and rest—you'll have fired all the ammo you previously collected.

# SUPPRESSED ASSAULT RIFLE

## EPIC
### SUPPRESSED ASSAULT RIFLE

**DAMAGE:** MID **FIRE RATE:** HIGH
**AMMO CAPACITY:** HIGH **RELOAD TIME:** LOW

**A SNEAKY ASSAULT RIFLE**

This helps you maintain your position in a stealthy manner. While you'd normally use an Assault Rifle in an open shootout, the Suppressed Assault Rifle is to be used more in line with other silenced weapons. Trigger tapping is encouraged.

## LEGENDARY
### SUPPRESSED ASSAULT RIFLE

**DAMAGE:** MID **FIRE RATE:** HIGH
**AMMO CAPACITY:** HIGH **RELOAD TIME:** LOW

**A SUPER-POWERED AND
QUIET ASSAULT RIFLE**

If a regular Assault Rifle won't do the job and you need to use stealth, this is your best bet. The Legendary variant of the Suppressed Assault Rifle deals solid damage and has a short reload time, so you can get in, grab some eliminations, and get out without being noticed.

# THERMAL SCOPED ASSAULT RIFLE

## EPIC
### THERMAL SCOPED ASSAULT RIFLE

**DAMAGE:** MID **FIRE RATE:** LOW
**AMMO CAPACITY:** MID
**RELOAD TIME:** LOW

**ILLUMINATE THE BATTLEFIELD WITH A HANDY THERMAL SCOPE**

This rifle rocks a high accuracy rate and an extremely powerful scope that enables you to scout out enemies and items you wouldn't be able to see otherwise by illuminating them in your sights. One advantage is that, no matter how far you are from your target, the damage remains consistent.

**FACT**
No one can hide from
the all-seeing eye of
the Thermal Scoped
Assault Rifle!

# LEGENDARY
## THERMAL SCOPED ASSAULT RIFLE

**DAMAGE:** MID **FIRE RATE:** LOW
**AMMO CAPACITY:** MID **RELOAD TIME:** LOW

### A SCOPED ASSAULT RIFLE PERFECT FOR FINDING AND ELIMINATING TARGETS ACROSS ANY TERRAIN

The Legendary Scoped Assault Rifle is a highly accurate weapon. It lets you take out enemies hidden in bushes, foliage, and other areas you wouldn't normally be able to see. However, despite its proficiency as a long-range weapon, you can use it as a normal assault rifle for medium- or close-range combat if you end up facing crowds of enemies.

## FACT
This weapon highlights various Llamas, Chests, Supply Drops, and other items in yellow.

# LIGHT MACHINE GUN

## RARE
### LIGHT MACHINE GUN

**DAMAGE:** LOW **FIRE RATE:** HIGH
**AMMO CAPACITY:** HIGH **RELOAD TIME:** HIGH

**A RAPID-FIRING AUTOMATIC WITH HIGH-CAPACITY MAGAZINE THAT'S GREAT UP CLOSE**

The Light Machine Gun's Rare variant is an excellent choice for players looking for a weapon with plenty of bullets and a high rate of fire at the same time. When fired in short bursts, it's far more accurate—hold the trigger too long and your shots will fly all over the place!

## FACT
The Rare Light Machine Gun is more powerful overall than the Legendary Assault Rifle, but less accurate.

35

**TIP**
Get up close and personal with the LMG—its high capacity makes it excellent for taking out nearby foes.

## EPIC
### LIGHT MACHINE GUN

**DAMAGE:** LOW **FIRE RATE:** HIGH
**AMMO CAPACITY:** HIGH **RELOAD TIME:** HIGH

**A DEVASTATING AUTOMATIC WEAPON THAT CAN EVEN TEAR THROUGH METAL WALLS**

The Light Machine Gun is a fantastic choice, especially with its Epic version. It's noisy, but also devastating, so even if you alert your opponents to your position, you may still be able to take 'em out with some quick moves. Light Machine Guns were eventually Vaulted at the start of Season 6.

# DRUM GUN

## UNCOMMON
### DRUM GUN

**DAMAGE:** LOW **FIRE RATE:** HIGH
**AMMO CAPACITY:** HIGH **RELOAD TIME:** MID

### AN SMG-TYPE WEAPON EFFECTIVE AT CLOSE AND MEDIUM RANGE

The Drum Gun has a striking appearance that's unlike any other weapon in Fortnite. It can be massively effective at close range, despite its lack of first-shot accuracy, and it can absolutely tear through just about anything at midrange. It may not hold up so well over longer distances, but it's still a formidable choice.

### FACT
The Drum Gun returned during the Unvaulting event at the end of Season 8.

# RARE
## DRUM GUN

**DAMAGE:** LOW **FIRE RATE:** HIGH
**AMMO CAPACITY:** HIGH
**RELOAD TIME:** MID

### A STRONG RIFLE-SMG HYBRID WITH SOME FANTASTIC CLOSE-RANGE ABILITIES

The already-powerful Drum Gun gets a big upgrade with its Rare variant. Best used in close- to midrange combat, it is a lower-tier machine gun that can hold tons of rounds of Medium Ammo. With a higher clip size and structural damage potential, it's often a popular choice among players who just want to cause chaos—and who can blame them?

# INFANTRY RIFLE

## COMMON
### INFANTRY RIFLE

**DAMAGE:** MID **FIRE RATE:** HIGH
**AMMO CAPACITY:** MID
**RELOAD TIME:** LOW

#### A SOLID ALLROUNDER

Designed for mid- to long-range use, this is a decent workhorse rifle, but don't get caught out by that slow reload time, while its lack of scope can make aiming tricky.

## UNCOMMON
### INFANTRY RIFLE

**DAMAGE:** MID **FIRE RATE:** HIGH
**AMMO CAPACITY:** MID
**RELOAD TIME:** LOW

#### MAKE EVERY SHOT COUNT

A curious member of the rifle family. You lose the ability to spray bullets at opponents, but skilled marksmen are able to dish out crazy damage even with this most basic version of the weapon.

## RARE
## INFANTRY RIFLE

**DAMAGE:** MID **FIRE RATE:** HIGH
**AMMO CAPACITY:** MID
**RELOAD TIME:** LOW

### UNLEASH THE BEAST

One tier of rarity can make all the difference. The damage boost this gun gets just allows it to down any opponent with two to the head and one to the body, meaning you only need to land two out of three crits. That extra leeway makes this gun way easier to use.

## EPIC
## INFANTRY RIFLE

**DAMAGE:** MID **FIRE RATE:** HIGH
**AMMO CAPACITY:** MID **RELOAD TIME:** LOW

### EVEN MORE BEASTLY

This is a hitscan weapon (meaning that bullets have no travel time or drop-off), so all you need to do is master finding the heads and taking the shot. Okay, it's not as easy as it sounds, but it sure is rewarding once you get it down.

# LEGENDARY
## INFANTRY RIFLE

**DAMAGE:** MID **FIRE RATE:** HIGH
**AMMO CAPACITY:** MID **RELOAD TIME:** LOW

### A TOP-TIER RIFLE, LOVED BY THE MASTERS

A lot of players have come to see the infantry rifle—and this top-end version in particular—as one of Fortnite's best weapons. It has an amazing effective range, awesome damage output, and respectable ammo economy. Best keep an automatic on hand to deal with close-quarters fights, though.

## FACT
The Epic and Legendary variants get an extra two shots per clip over the others, allowing for sustained pressure.

# TACTICAL ASSAULT RIFLE

## RARE
### TACTICAL ASSAULT RIFLE

**DAMAGE:** LOW **FIRE RATE:** HIGH
**AMMO CAPACITY:** HIGH **RELOAD TIME:** LOW

### HANDY IN A TIGHT SPOT

Somewhere between a SMG and an assault rifle, this is a smart choice for close-quarters combat. Firing seven bullets per second, this is currently the third fastest assault rifle in the game—happily it has a decent ammo capacity.

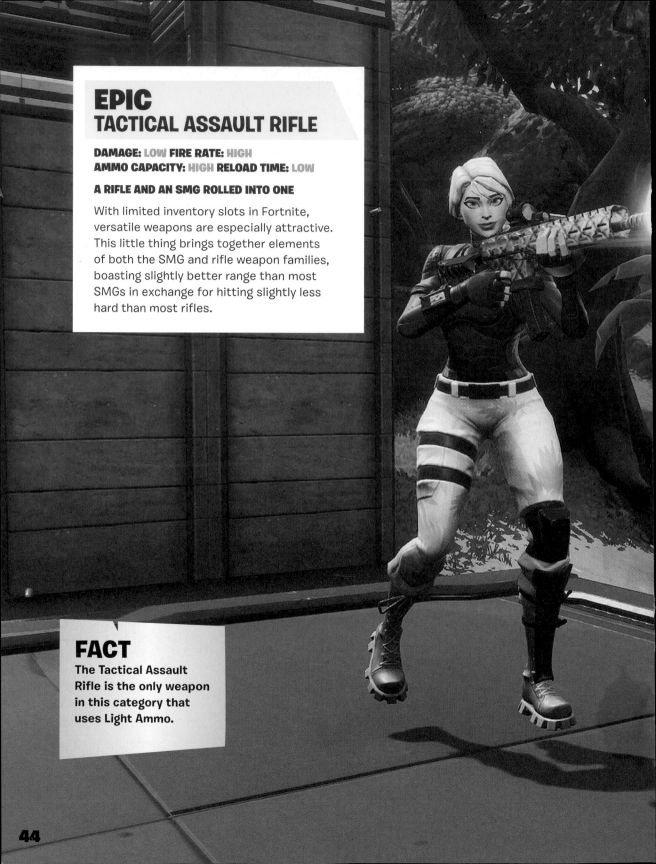

# EPIC
## TACTICAL ASSAULT RIFLE

**DAMAGE:** LOW **FIRE RATE:** HIGH
**AMMO CAPACITY:** HIGH **RELOAD TIME:** LOW

### A RIFLE AND AN SMG ROLLED INTO ONE

With limited inventory slots in Fortnite, versatile weapons are especially attractive. This little thing brings together elements of both the SMG and rifle weapon families, boasting slightly better range than most SMGs in exchange for hitting slightly less hard than most rifles.

## FACT
The Tactical Assault Rifle is the only weapon in this category that uses Light Ammo.

# LEGENDARY
## TACTICAL ASSAULT RIFLE

**DAMAGE:** LOW **FIRE RATE:** HIGH
**AMMO CAPACITY:** HIGH **RELOAD TIME:** LOW

### BACKUP WEAPONS DON'T COME MUCH BETTER

The Tactical AR isn't likely to be many players' first choice as a main weapon. But as a secondary option to pull out when you need to finish someone off, this little bullet hose is well up there with the best. Fast fire rate and reload speeds mean it's always ready to go.

## GOOD THINGS COME
## IN SMALL PACKAGES

Don't waste time searching for a boomstick before you start to throw down in a match. If anything, you're better off getting the jump on opponents as soon as you have a pistol—take them out with whatever you find before they have chance to gear up, and your life will be much easier!

# UNVAULTED

## A LIMITED TIME MODE WHERE JUST ABOUT ANYTHING GOES!

Did you miss out on certain weapons and items seen previously in Fortnite? Turn back the clock with the Unvaulted game mode, which lets you open a portal into the past to see some of the awesome toys that have come and gone. They may have been removed from Battle Royale, but that doesn't mean they're lost forever—just hit up this mode for a quick, retro-tinged look at the good old days when the Bouncers reigned supreme. You never quite know what might turn up when you explore this mode, so we're going to take a look at what makes it such a cool addition to the game. Get ready for some flashbacks!

# RECONNECT WITH OLD FRIENDS

The main point of Unvaulted is to let players spend some time with the weapons and items they thought they might never get to see again. Rotating things in and out like this is a good way to let you use everything in the game, without compromising the competitive nature of the core Battle Royale mode. If there's a weapon that you really miss adding to your arsenal, you may still be able to play with it in Unvaulted.

# SEE HOW FORTNITE HAS CHANGED

Unvaulted is a great way to look into the past to see how the game has evolved. Think of it as a playable time capsule—maybe you missed some of the weapons and items that weren't in the game for long. Or perhaps there's a particular weapon from an older season that you really wanted to try out. Now's your chance!

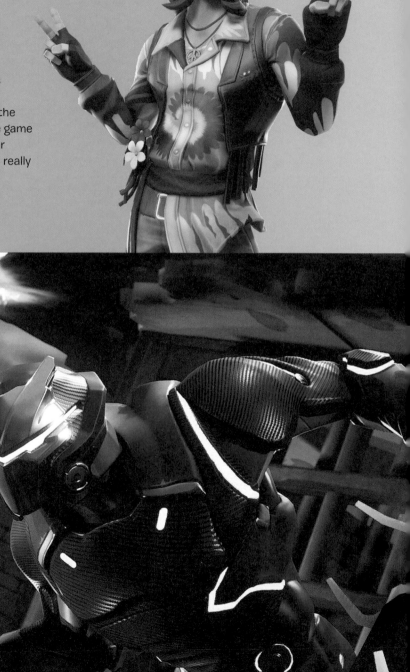

# GET SOME PRACTICE IN

Just because an item has been Vaulted, it doesn't mean you're never going to see it again. Unvaulted offers a way for you to get some practice with weapons and goodies that you may never have otherwise touched, so when they're back in the game you know exactly what you're doing.

# VARIETY IS THE SPICE OF LIFE

We all love to see some variety from time to time. While Fortnite always keeps us guessing, sometimes it's fun to sprinkle other interesting things into the mix that will only be available for a short period. Unvaulted gives us a bit of a change of pace without throwing us into a new battlefield like a seasonal event.

# PUMPED FULL OF POWER

**AN EXPLOSIVE SOLUTION TO CLOSE COMBAT, THESE HAVE THE POTENTIAL TO END FACE-TO-FACE ENCOUNTERS**

Shotguns are the masters of burst damage, allowing players to dominate skirmishes at close quarters with a high degree of control and stopping power. Each one boasts an impressive capacity to down enemies quickly, and their potential to dish out critical damage with headshots is something to be feared. Many top streamers have shown how effective these weapons are at controlling tight spaces and winning build fights by constantly pushing and closing the gap.

While shotguns do well up close, they suffer when it comes to fighting over longer distances, and can be inconsistent in the damage they dish out.

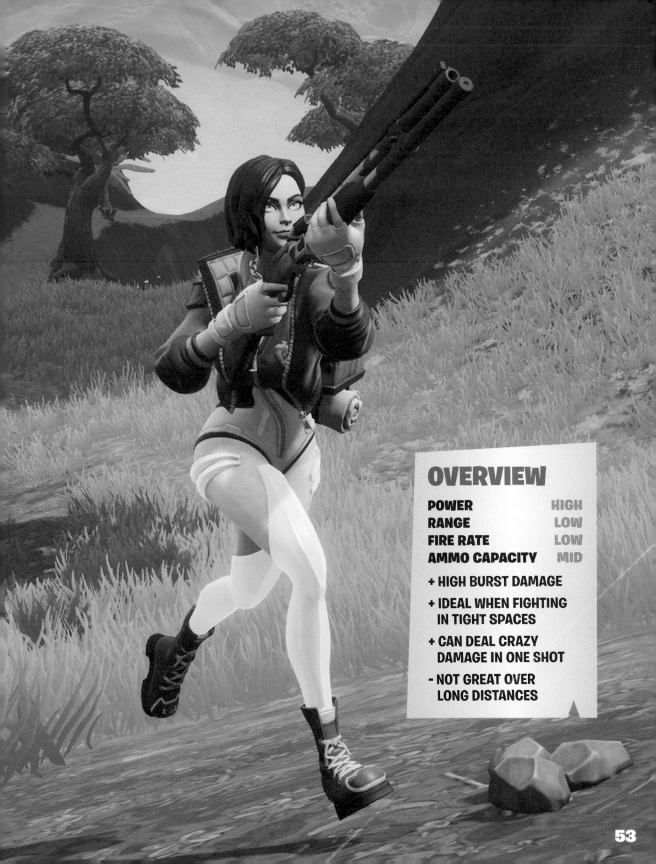

## OVERVIEW

| | |
|---|---|
| POWER | HIGH |
| RANGE | LOW |
| FIRE RATE | LOW |
| AMMO CAPACITY | MID |

+ HIGH BURST DAMAGE

+ IDEAL WHEN FIGHTING IN TIGHT SPACES

+ CAN DEAL CRAZY DAMAGE IN ONE SHOT

- NOT GREAT OVER LONG DISTANCES

## EPIC
### DOUBLE BARREL SHOTGUN

**DAMAGE:** HIGH **FIRE RATE:** LOW
**AMMO CAPACITY:** LOW **RELOAD TIME:** MID

#### TWO SHOTS FOR THE PRICE OF ONE

With its short effective range, this twin-chambered firearm requires you to get up close and personal to make the most of its potential. Those who master it, however, will be able to dish out a huge amount of double barrel damage.

# LEGENDARY
## DOUBLE BARREL SHOTGUN

**DAMAGE:** HIGH **FIRE RATE:** LOW
**AMMO CAPACITY:** LOW **RELOAD TIME:** MID

### BIG TROUBLE CRAMMED INTO A SMALL PACKAGE

This beast is often considered to be somewhat risky, as its low ammo capacity leaves very little room for error, but it undeniably offers a huge payoff if you land your shots. As such, the Double Barrel Shotgun is perfect for going up against single opponents in close quarters.

# HEAVY SHOTGUN

## EPIC
### HEAVY SHOTGUN

**DAMAGE:** HIGH **FIRE RATE:** MID
**AMMO CAPACITY:** MID
**RELOAD TIME:** HIGH

#### OVERWHELM OPPONENTS WITH THIS HEAVY HITTER

Striking a balance between the other shotgun variants, the Epic Heavy Shotgun offers the best of both worlds—it hits hard and fast. With a reasonable fire rate and respectable damage, it can capably handle most medium- and short-range fights, making it ideal for fighting solo or in duos.

# LEGENDARY
## HEAVY SHOTGUN

**DAMAGE:** HIGH **FIRE RATE:** MID
**AMMO CAPACITY:** MID **RELOAD TIME:** HIGH

### CRUSH THE OPPOSITION UNDER THE WEIGHT OF THIS MONSTER

With its high damage and decent fire rate, the Heavy Shotgun makes for an ideal tool to smash through any close-quarters encounters. This particular one shines, however, because it functions well over medium distances, too, allowing players to continue dealing damage even when the combat starts to split apart.

> "A GOLDEN START WITH THE BEST WEAPON IN THE GAME!"
> TFUE

7 | 0

0 | 100
100 | 100

MEMORY USED

32.743 | 100.000

# PUMP SHOTGUN

## UNCOMMON
### PUMP SHOTGUN

**DAMAGE:** HIGH **FIRE RATE:** LOW
**AMMO CAPACITY:** MID
**RELOAD TIME:** HIGH

### NOT YOUR EVERYDAY BOOMSTICK

The Uncommon Pump Shotgun is the fan favorite for duos or teams. This is thanks largely to its high spawn frequency and sheer destructive power. It can be used to put pressure on opposing players bunkered behind structures, while allies hang back to finish off any stragglers.

# RARE
## PUMP SHOTGUN

**DAMAGE:** HIGH **FIRE RATE:** LOW
**AMMO CAPACITY:** MID **RELOAD TIME:** HIGH

### SHOOTING STRAIGHT TOWARDS
### THAT VICTORY ROYALE

The popular Rare Pump Shotgun enables a perfect
headshot, with all pellets making contact to instantly
down an enemy from full health. Awesome—but
remember that, as with other pump shotguns, it's
noisy and has a low fire rate that can leave you
vulnerable to enemy attention.

# EPIC
## PUMP SHOTGUN

**DAMAGE:** HIGH **FIRE RATE:** LOW
**AMMO CAPACITY:** MID **RELOAD TIME:** MID

### BLAST PAST YOUR FOES IN STYLE

The Epic Pump Shotgun is a later addition to the shotgun family. Introduced as an alternative to the coveted Heavy Shotgun, this option is perfect for ripping a large amount of health from an opponent with just a single shot, allowing you to quickly swap to another weapon with a faster rate of fire to finish them off without too much trouble.

## TIP
Use the shotgun's pellet spread to catch out fleeing enemies. You don't need to be super-precise with this gun!

# LEGENDARY
## PUMP SHOTGUN

**DAMAGE:** HIGH **FIRE RATE:** LOW
**AMMO CAPACITY:** MID **RELOAD TIME:** MID

### PUSHING THE PUMP TO ITS LIMITS

The Legendary Pump Shotgun boasts the highest
single shot damage of the shotgun family. While
you may not see it too often on the battlefield,
this powerhouse can stop a player in their tracks
with its potential to deal more damage than the
maximum health and shield values combined.

## FACT
The Legendary Pump
Shotgun does a mighty
110 maximum damage,
making it an incredibly
potent weapon.

# TACTICAL SHOTGUN

## COMMON
### TACTICAL SHOTGUN

**DAMAGE:** HIGH **FIRE RATE:** MID
**AMMO CAPACITY:** MID **RELOAD TIME:** HIGH

**THE TRIED-AND-TRUE TECHNIQUE TO WINNING**

The Common Tactical Shotgun is the perfect companion to run alongside a secondary weapon like an SMG or Assault Rifle. With a similar range to that of the Heavy Shotgun, the Tactical alternative gives you the flexibility to fight over medium distances.

## UNCOMMON
### TACTICAL SHOTGUN

**DAMAGE:** HIGH **FIRE RATE:** LOW
**AMMO CAPACITY:** MID **RELOAD TIME:** HIGH

**THE VERSATILE OPTION FOR ANY SITUATION**

The Uncommon Tactical Shotgun is a reliable weapon to have tucked away in your pocket. With an effective range longer than that of the Pump Shotgun, this versatile weapon is great for adapting to different situations.

# RARE
## TACTICAL SHOTGUN

**DAMAGE:** HIGH **FIRE RATE:** MID
**AMMO CAPACITY:** MID **RELOAD TIME:** HIGH

### A TACTICAL TOOL TO TAKE THE WIN

This is a respectable weapon that fits well in most arsenals thanks to its high rate of fire and damage output. The Tactical Shotgun's speed makes this weapon a monster. With the fastest fire rate of the original roster of shotties, the Rare Tactical Shotgun is one of the most forgiving options available.

"I LIKE THE WAY IT FEELS. I CAN GET UP IN THEIR FACE AND NOT HAVE TO WORRY ABOUT IT."
**NINJA**

# COMBAT SHOTGUN

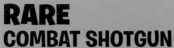

## RARE
### COMBAT SHOTGUN

**DAMAGE:** HIGH **FIRE RATE:** MID
**AMMO CAPACITY:** MID **RELOAD TIME:** HIGH

**BUILT TO GO THE DISTANCE**

Range is the primary weakness of the shotgun family, but this weapon bucks that trend spectacularly. A tight pellet spread makes it harder to land close-range shots than with any other shotgun, but allows this unique weapon to land a lot of damage from much greater distances.

# EPIC
## COMBAT SHOTGUN

**DAMAGE:** HIGH **FIRE RATE:** MID
**AMMO CAPACITY:** MID **RELOAD TIME:** HIGH

### PEPPER OPPONENTS FROM DOWNTOWN WITH THIS BEAST

Shotgun duels are a pretty common occurrence in Fortnite, and this is among the trickier tools to use in a close-range blast-off. In any other kind of encounter, however, this things can shred opponents from crazy distances, with a combination of concentrated projectiles and low damage drop-off that allows it to outrange any other shotgun.

## LEGENDARY
### COMBAT SHOTGUN

**DAMAGE:** HIGH **FIRE RATE:** MID
**AMMO CAPACITY:** MID **RELOAD TIME:** HIGH

#### NOW THAT'S A BOOMSTICK...

Is there anything this monster weapon can't do?
Well, yes—while its range and fire rate make it an
absolute menace at midrange, its tight spread
pattern requires a lot more precision than your
typical shotgun. Master that, though, and this is
one of the scariest weapons in the game.

### FACT
The Legendary variant
does a flat 50 damage
to structures, making it
a useful tool for speedy
and efficient demolition.

## KNOWLEDGE IS POWER!

## NEVER BE AFRAID TO BE A BIT DIFFERENT

It can be all too easy to fall into the trap of thinking that only certain weapons—especially those preferred by some pros and streamers—are worth looking out for. One of the best things about Fortnite, though, is that just about everything is viable in the right hands, so try it all out and see what works best for you!

# RIDERS ON THE STORM

## WHY WALK WHEN YOU CAN CRUISE AROUND THE ISLAND IN STYLE?

When there's a storm brewing and you need to be somewhere fast, try to find a ride. Gliders were the only way to get around quickly in Fortnite's first three seasons, but additional mobility tools have been added in every season since, which make each drop onto the island that much more interesting. Just as you need to learn where the loot hotspots are, it's now also a good idea to get accustomed to where vehicles typically spawn. Here are some of the alternate modes of travel recently found in the game, so be sure to keep a lookout for them next time you jump out of the Battle Bus.

# SHOPPING CART

**INTRODUCED IN:** SEASON 4
**SEATS:** 2
**DURABILITY:** LOW
**SPEED:** LOW

Fortnite's first vehicle came creaking onto the scene in Season 4. While it may not look very effective, this cart can be a beast in the right hands. It's capable of picking up a fair amount of speed when going downhill—you can even build your own ramps to make use of this fact—and it protects riders from a degree of fall damage, making it possible to perform some insane jumps and stunts.

# BALLER

**INTRODUCED IN:** SEASON 8
**SEATS:** 1
**DURABILITY:** LOW
**SPEED:** MEDIUM/HIGH

This orb-shaped oddity rolled out just two weeks into Season 8, and it changed the game overnight. With its built-in grappling hook, the Baller can get you to places no other land vehicle can, and its erratic movement makes it much harder for enemies to hit, too. Combine the boost with the grapple to get insane air and you'll be able to get across the island in no time.

# ALL TERRAIN KART

**INTRODUCED IN:** SEASON 5
**SEATS:** 4
**DURABILITY:** MEDIUM
**SPEED:** MEDIUM

This golf buggy is the perfect ride when touching down as a team. The driver has to focus on getting from A to B, but anyone else riding along is free to build and use weapons and items, all while getting around the map that much faster and with a degree of protection. Ferrying around an entire squad is extremely useful.

# QUADCRASHER

**INTRODUCED IN: SEASON 6**
**SEATS: 2**
**DURABILITY: MEDIUM**
**SPEED: MEDIUM/HIGH**

This is effectively an upgraded version of the ATK, trading subtlety for destructive power. It only seats two players, but its enhancements make it worth that trade-off. Boosters refill quickly, and the plow-like wedge on the front allows it to tear through most structures at full speed.

# X-4 STORMWING

**INTRODUCED IN: SEASON 7**
**SEATS: 5**
**DURABILITY: HIGH**
**SPEED: HIGH**

This is the absolute pinnacle of vehicular travel in Fortnite. This biplane lets you soar over the island and take the fight to opponents from the skies. One allied daredevil can take to each wing for a total of five players on board. Wing-riders get to use their weapons as usual and can leap off whenever they like to glide back into the fray, and the pilot even has access to a powerful mounted machine gun. A great way to get the advantage on your foes.

# DRIFTBOARD

**INTRODUCED IN: SEASON 7**
**SEATS: 1**
**DURABILITY: MEDIUM**
**SPEED: MEDIUM**

If you want to style your way across the island, this will certainly be your ride of choice. Boosters allow it to reach surprising speeds, which can be combined with a chargeable jump to catch serious air. While you're up there, be sure to bust out your best tricks, but make sure you nail the landing—nobody is going to be impressed if you hit the ground face-first.

# GLIDER

**INTRODUCED IN:** SEASON 1
**SEATS:** 1
**DURABILITY:** LOW
**SPEED:** MEDIUM

Technically you start every game with a vehicle—your Glider. It's a more efficient way of getting around than on foot, although you can only make use of it after the initial drop if you manage to find reserves around the island. If you do, make liberal use of Rifts, Bouncers, structures, and anything else that might give you a chance to get some air.

# ROAD TRIP! WHY VEHICLES ARE SO MUCH BETTER WITH FRIENDS

While playing solo, think long and hard about taking a vehicle. Sure, they can be great for covering long distances, but if you think you can make it on foot, you're often going to be safer doing so. Vehicles are typically loud and can leave their drivers defenseless, so you might end up being the center of attention if you choose to catch a ride. When playing in groups, however, vehicles become much more important. Being able to move a squad around quickly lets you travel to and loot areas that are way out of the Battle Bus's path, and the use of transport either gets you out of trouble in a hurry or lets you start it just as fast.

# SMALL BUT MIGHTY

## FROM LONG-RANGE BEASTS TO UP-CLOSE SILENT ASSASSINS, PISTOLS OFFER A TON OF VARIETY

Handguns may not always be the most sought-after weapons in the world of Fortnite—but they may just be some of the most versatile. Some can take down full shields from across the map with one shot. Others will rip right through you if you are stupid enough to stand right in front of them. Some even come in pairs. It may mean that you can't rely on all handguns to do the same job, but it does mean that having a selection of them available to you in the early game can often be a better situation than only finding launchers or snipers. You just have to know how to use them well. Often overlooked, handguns can in fact be game-changing weapons, and there is a lot more to them than you might think.

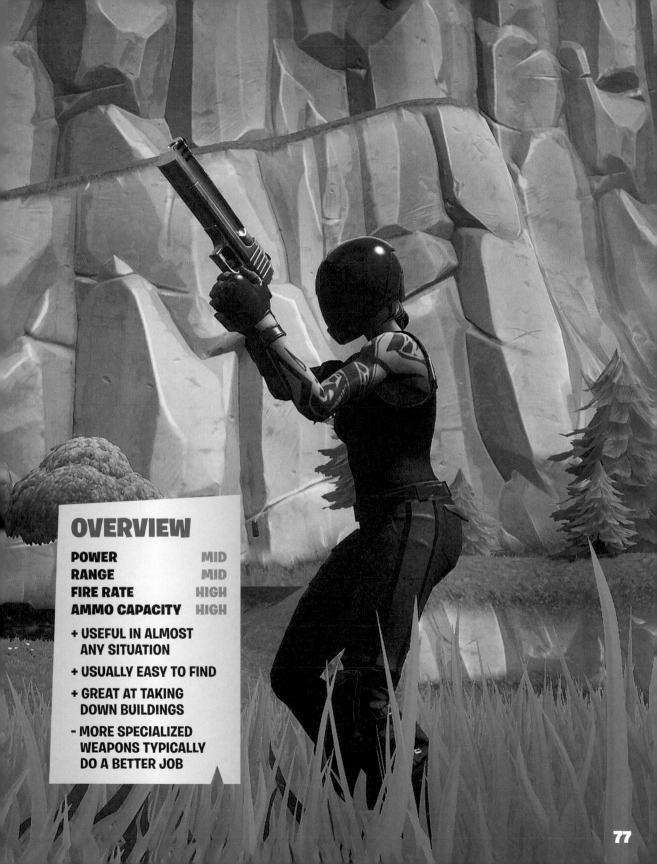

## OVERVIEW

| | |
|---|---|
| POWER | MID |
| RANGE | MID |
| FIRE RATE | HIGH |
| AMMO CAPACITY | HIGH |

+ USEFUL IN ALMOST ANY SITUATION

+ USUALLY EASY TO FIND

+ GREAT AT TAKING DOWN BUILDINGS

- MORE SPECIALIZED WEAPONS TYPICALLY DO A BETTER JOB

# HAND CANNON

# EPIC
## HAND CANNON

**DAMAGE:** HIGH **FIRE RATE:** LOW
**AMMO CAPACITY:** LOW **RELOAD TIME:** LOW

### THE ONE-SHOT WONDER

When it comes to handguns, the Hand Cannon is by far the hardest hitter. One headshot will take out an opponent with up to half shields, and two headshots will down anyone. The power this thing kicks out is simply unmatched by any other handgun, and all you need to do is hit one headshot to win almost every fight. If you are confident of hitting your shots and not needing to spray bullets to try and connect with your target, the Hand Cannon is almost a must-have.

# LEGENDARY
## HAND CANNON

**DAMAGE:** HIGH **FIRE RATE:** LOW
**AMMO CAPACITY:** LOW **RELOAD TIME:** LOW

### BREAK THE WALLS DOWN!

This is the top-tier handgun in almost all
situations. Up close, it rips through foes
that are unlucky enough to get in the way,
and at range, it is almost like a Sniper Rifle.
But it is also great at destroying buildings,
with a ridiculously high structure damage.
In duos or squads, you can combo this with
a launcher that your squadmate fires.

## COMMON
### PISTOL

**DAMAGE:** LOW **FIRE RATE:** HIGH
**AMMO CAPACITY:** MID **RELOAD TIME:** LOW

#### OLD RELIABLE STILL HAS A PLACE

Chances are you have ignored the Common Pistol more times than you have picked it up. It has low damage, almost every other weapon seems better in more situations, and it is visually less exciting than many other options. Sure, it may not be the most inspiring choice, but if you have a quick trigger finger, then it can deal a lot of damage in a short period.

## FACT
A Common Pistol only does slightly less damage per second less than a Common Suppressed SMG.

**TIP**
If you're firing a pistol at mid- to long-range, then remember to pause slightly between shots for the best accuracy.

# UNCOMMON
## PISTOL

**DAMAGE:** LOW **FIRE RATE:** HIGH
**AMMO CAPACITY:** MID **RELOAD TIME:** LOW

### QUICK TRIGGER FINGERS WIN VICTORY ROYALES

Since day one, shotguns have been the go-to for close-range combat. But if you look at the stats, the Uncommon Pistol can do just as well in the same situations. It all comes down to fire rates: the humble Pistol can fire around five times faster than, say, a Tactical Shotgun. That means that if you are fighting against someone with a shotgun and they miss their first shot, you have many more chances to bring them down.

## RARE
### PISTOL

**DAMAGE:** LOW **FIRE RATE:** HIGH
**AMMO CAPACITY:** MID **RELOAD TIME:** LOW

### A HANDY HEAVY HITTER

Unfortunately the Rare Pistol is no more, having been removed entirely from the game. But when it was around, it was perhaps the only pistol choice you would realistically consider taking over other weapons. The slight damage increase meant this could two-shot someone with no shields, which is a big advantage over the other two pistol variants.

# REVOLVER

## TIP

The Revolver is capable of one-shotting unshielded opponents, making it a great early-game weapon.

## COMMON
### REVOLVER

**DAMAGE:** MID **FIRE RATE:** LOW
**AMMO CAPACITY:** LOW **RELOAD TIME:** LOW

#### HIGH RISK, HIGH REWARDS

The Revolver is one of the most divisive weapons in all of Fortnite. Some players love to use them, as the high headshot damage rewards accurate players. Others, meanwhile, avoid it at all costs, thinking there's always a better option. The main problem is when you miss a shot mid-fight, as a slow fire rate and low ammo capacity mean that mistakes can cost you dearly.

# UNCOMMON
## REVOLVER

**DAMAGE:** MID **FIRE RATE:** LOW
**AMMO CAPACITY:** LOW **RELOAD TIME:** LOW

### SOMEONE CALL A DOCTOR

Although he didn't always opt for this weapon, popular streamer Dr. Lupo would often pick up a Revolver to pull off some crazy trickshots. There are multiple clips of him making impressive plays with the weapon, from long-range snipes to close-range reaction headshots, sometimes flicking from one head to another in a no more than a second.

"I LOVE REVOLVERS, SO MUCH. THEY ARE SO GOOD!"
DR. LUPO

# RARE
## REVOLVER

**DAMAGE:** MID **FIRE RATE:** LOW
**AMMO CAPACITY:** LOW **RELOAD TIME:** LOW

### A HAND CANNON FROM YESTERYEAR

The ammo capacity may be quite low on this Revolver, but it still has a good kick to it, capable of dealing out 60 damage. As ever, a good headshot will make all the difference when wielding this weapon, but don't be caught out by the comparatively slow reload time.

## FACT
Headshots from Revolvers can do over 100 damage at close range. That makes them handy for getting in some impressive one-shot eliminations early on.

# SIX SHOOTER

## UNCOMMON
### SIX SHOOTER

**DAMAGE:** MID **FIRE RATE:** MID
**AMMO CAPACITY:** LOW **RELOAD TIME:** MID

### ISN'T THAT JUST THE REVOLVER?

The Six Shooter looks almost the same as the old
Revolver, just with a new paint job and amazing equip
animation. For the most part it is very similar, but the
key change here is that you can rapid-fire with the Six
Shooter when firing from the hip. You can quickly slam
out six bullets at point-blank range, which will usually
eliminate just about anyone.

> "JUST LOOK AT
> HOW DOPE IT
> LOOKS WHEN
> YOU PULL [THE
> SIX SHOOTER]
> OUT! WOOHOO,
> LOOK AT THAT!"
> HAMLINZ

**TIP**
The Hand Cannon can take down a half-shielded foe in one headshot, even at range, whereas the Rare Six Shooter needs to hit three times.

# RARE
## SIX SHOOTER

**DAMAGE:** MID **FIRE RATE:** MID
**AMMO CAPACITY:** LOW
**RELOAD TIME:** LOW

### RAPID-FIRE TO VICTORY

Being able to fire rapidly at close range makes the Six Shooter way more viable than the Revolver in a lot of situations. However, the reduced damage means this is less effective as a long-range weapon. It still has solid accuracy when aiming down the sights, but it takes more bullets to drop foes at long range. This means you have to hit more difficult shots, making the Hand Cannon a much better Sniper replacement than the Six Shooter.

## EPIC
## SIX SHOOTER

**DAMAGE:** MID **FIRE RATE:** MID
**AMMO CAPACITY:** LOW **RELOAD TIME:** LOW

### SIX SHOTS MEANS SIX DOWNS, RIGHT?

If you expect a lot of fighting at close
range then the Epic Six Shooter is a vital
part of your arsenal. Pair it with a Shotgun
and you can drop anyone simply by landing
right next to them. Lead with a Shotgun
blast and then switch to the Six Shooter
and rapid-fire all six bullets at them to
secure the elimination.

### TIP
The Epic Six Shooter
has the highest damage
per second of all
handguns, just beating
out the Legendary
Suppressed Pistol.

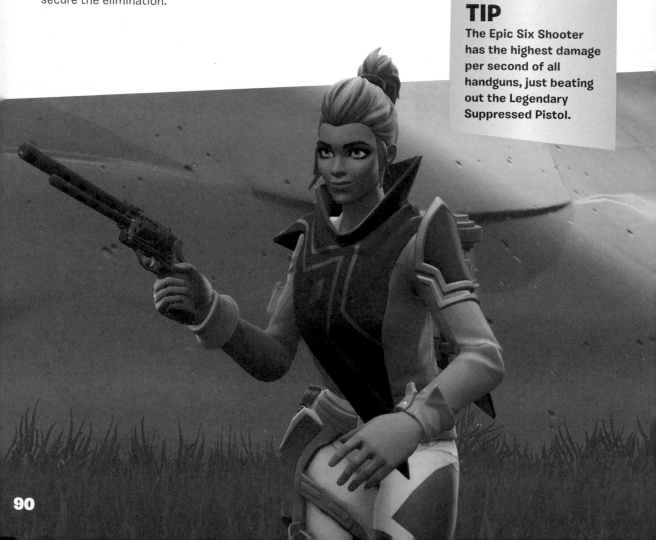

# SUPPRESSED PISTOL

## RARE
### SUPPRESSED PISTOL

**DAMAGE:** LOW **FIRE RATE:** HIGH
**AMMO CAPACITY:** MID **RELOAD TIME:** LOW

### THE QUIET RIOT

It turns out that sticking a silencer on the Pistol and giving it slightly more damage makes it a much more viable weapon. A great fire rate and decent ammo capacity means that you can fire a load of bullets off in quick succession. This is great for starting a fight when you haven't been spotted, as you can easily get a good chunk of damage done before your enemy knows what's hit them.

<blockquote>
**"I THINK THE SUPPRESSED PISTOL IS ONE OF THE BEST BACKUP WEAPONS IN THE GAME FOR ANY DISTANCE."**
DRIFTOR
</blockquote>

# EPIC
## SUPPRESSED PISTOL

**DAMAGE:** LOW **FIRE RATE:** HIGH
**AMMO CAPACITY:** MID **RELOAD TIME:** LOW

### THE SOUND OF SILENCE

Chances are you're never going to use this as your main weapon past the mid-game, but as something to start and finish a fight, it's great. If you miss a couple of Shotgun blasts then the Suppressed Pistol is a great option to pull out and fire until you take down your foe. A similar thing can be done at longer range with an Assault Rifle if you have solid aim. If you are really good, you can try and pair it with a Sniper Rifle to finish off someone who you just managed to tag.

# DUAL PISTOLS

## RARE
### DUAL PISTOLS

**DAMAGE:** MID **FIRE RATE:** MID
**AMMO CAPACITY:** MID **RELOAD TIME:** MID

### YOU'VE GOT TWO HANDS...MIGHT AS WELL USE THEM BOTH, RIGHT?

What's better than one pistol? Two, of course. A single press of the trigger fires both weapons, delivering a powerful punch. If you're able to consistently hit headshots, they are often far too powerful for your foe. It was a big reason why these ended up in the Vault for a time, as they can deal huge amounts of damage in the right hands.

## TIP

Dual Pistols are extremely good at taking down buildings, as they are able to deliver surprisingly high environmental damage.

## EPIC
### DUAL PISTOLS

**DAMAGE:** MID **FIRE RATE:** MID
**AMMO CAPACITY:** MID **RELOAD TIME:** MID

### DUAL WIELDING MAKES YOU AWESOME. FACT!

As you might expect when holding an entire pistol with just one hand, recoil is a pretty big issue when using the Dual Pistols. However, once you learn that aiming lower and then letting the kick of the guns carry shots upwards is a solid tactic when in a close-range fight, you realize the power of the weapon.

# FLINT-KNOCK PISTOL

## COMMON
### FLINT-KNOCK PISTOL

**DAMAGE:** HIGH **FIRE RATE:** LOW
**AMMO CAPACITY:** LOW **RELOAD TIME:** MID

### RECOIL ISN'T ALWAYS A BAD THING

The Flint-Knock Pistol might seem like a poor man's Hand Cannon on paper, but it has a unique side effect that makes it useful in its own regard. Firing the gun's single chambered shot creates a crazy amount of knockback—enough to send you flying skywards or to prevent fall damage if aimed downward. Just as effective for getting the high ground as it is for blasting enemies.

## UNCOMMON
### FLINT-KNOCK PISTOL

**DAMAGE:** HIGH **FIRE RATE:** LOW
**AMMO CAPACITY:** LOW **RELOAD TIME:** MID

### A GUN THAT FIRES POSITIONAL ADVANTAGES

While this strange weapon might be best used for getting around, its damage potential is certainly nothing to be scoffed at, either. A single headshot can eliminate more or less anyone who isn't at full shields, although you only get one chance to land that crucial shot before needing to switch weapons or sitting through the reload time.

# KNOWLEDGE IS POWER!

## MIND GAMES CAN BE THE ULTIMATE WEAPON!

Crazy costumes, distracting dances, and other off-putting behavior can all be effective tools in your quest for victory. If you can get inside an opponent's head, you can often force mistakes or hesitation, buying you a moment to push the advantage. Get weird and wonderful if you want to win big!

# GEARING UP

With so many different weapons, strategies, and play styles in Fortnite, it pays to be equipped to deal with anything. That means finding a lot of gear, so you're going to need to know where to look if you want to stock up on useful equipment and items as quickly as possible. There are a ton of ways to add to your arsenal, and each has its own benefits and drawbacks. Here are the most common places where you can grab new gear, along with everything you need to know about each different loot source.

# CHESTS

Treasure chests will be a common option for stocking up in most games, since they're fairly plentiful and tend to contain a selection of decent gear. As well as weapons, they also contain useful stuff like ammo, building materials, and consumables, and the odds of getting rare loot from a chest are usually a fair bit higher than with the floor loot that litters the island. There are loads of possible chest spawns on the map, but only a handful are active in each session—use Playground mode to scout all possible chest locations, since they're all up at once in this noncompetitive mode.

# ON THE GROUND

This is the most common place to find loot, but the loot itself is also common. The chances of finding an Epic or better weapon just sitting on the floor are extremely low, so be sure to grab them when you see them, if only to prevent other players from getting their hands on them. A lot of the more powerful weapons and items (such as Rocket Launchers and Chug Jugs) are not included in the pool of possible loot that can just be found lying around, so you'll still need to be popping open containers wherever you find them if you want the best chance of survival.

# SUPPLY DROPS

These crates packed with goodies are not only one of the most iconic loot sources in Fortnite, but also among the most lucrative. With a great chance to find high-end weapons and items in bulk, it's no surprise that players often go out of their way to chase these balloon-carried containers and reap the rewards. But therein lies the greatest risk with Supply Drops—they're flagged up on the map and quite often contested or camped out by opposing players, so cracking them open can be dangerous. Check your surroundings and throw up some defenses before you go in for them.

## FACT
Supply Drops come much more frequently in Large Team Modes, so take some backup and go crack a few open!

# BURIED TREASURE

A throwback to Season 8, when pirates ruled the island. The concept of the Buried Treasure item has also been used in several Limited Time Modes. Equipping the map item creates a trail to follow, with a large X on the ground when you reach your destination. Dig out the chest with your Harvesting Tool and you'll typically find enough top-end gear to outfit an entire squad. The downside here is that the route you need to follow is completely random, and could lead you into enemy territory or the path of the Storm. If you can reach the buried loot quickly and safely, though, it's always worth going for.

# LOOT CARRIERS

Season 9 introduced Hot Spots, highlighted named locations with a greater loot density than usual. Most of this extra gear is carried by these flying drones, and you'll need to shoot them down and grab whatever goodies they drop when destroyed. Of course, doing so will give away your position so there's always risk involved, but there tends to be quite a few of these about so you can usually get your hands on a couple of Carriers' worth of gear before making a getaway so long as you move fast. Like Supply Drops, Hot Spots are clearly visible on the map, so you should always expect to have company.

# ELIMINATED PLAYERS

Downing a rival causes them to drop everything, which can often be quite a haul towards the end of a game. This makes eliminating others one of the best ways to get your hands on a lot of gear. Keep an eye out for groups of players already battling it out, since you can sometimes swoop in to clean up when any survivors are weakened or distracted. Although this can be a great way to gear up, don't get greedy—retreating players could be leading you into a trap or back to their allies.

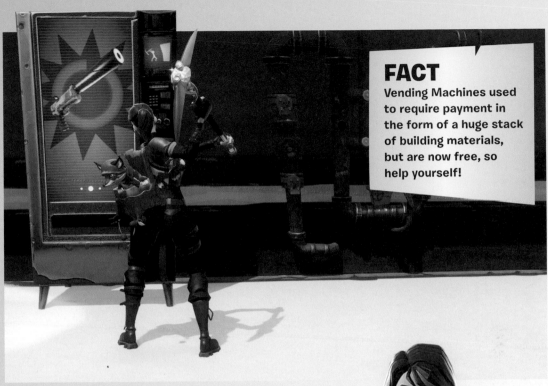

# VENDING MACHINES

The great thing about these free loot contraptions is that you can see from a distance roughly how good their contents will be based on the color. It's unlikely to be worth risking your life for a blue vending machine, for instance, but a Legendary one might offer you a game-changing item. Each Vending Machine contains three items selected at random. You can cycle through these more quickly with a quick swipe of your Harvesting Tool, then all you need to do is interact with the machine when it displays the item you want.

# RAPID-FIRE REAPERS

## LOW-DAMAGE BUT QUICK-FIRING GUNS THAT CAN CHALLENGE SHOTGUNS FOR THE TITLE OF "BEST SHORT-RANGE OPTION"

In a game where you are just as likely to be fighting someone meters away as you are someone in the distance, having a close-range weapon or two is always a solid idea, and submachine guns (SMGs) are perfect for that. Their lack of accuracy and range make them poor for long-distance encounters, but they will rip through anyone foolish enough to get too close. Most also have large ammo capacity, affording more chances to hit.

If you find yourself in a build battle, an SMG will not only be great for short-range engagement, but also at tearing through whatever your opponent has made.

## OVERVIEW

| | |
|---|---|
| **POWER** | LOW |
| **RANGE** | LOW |
| **FIRE RATE** | HIGH |
| **AMMO CAPACITY** | MID |

+ AMAZING UP CLOSE

+ GREAT FOR BRINGING
  DOWN BUILDINGS

+ SOLID ACCURACY

- LOW BASE DAMAGE

# SUBMACHINE GUN

## COMMON
### SUBMACHINE GUN

**DAMAGE:** LOW **FIRE RATE:** HIGH
**AMMO CAPACITY:** HIGH **RELOAD TIME:** MID

**IF AT FIRST YOU DON'T SUCCEED...**

The latest version of the Common Submachine Gun is the result of many attempts at creating a bullet hose that feels powerful in the correct situation, but not too strong elsewhere. Low damage per shot but a high rate of fire and solid ammo capacity make this great if you are confident of hitting every bullet.

# UNCOMMON
## SUBMACHINE GUN

**DAMAGE:** LOW **FIRE RATE:** HIGH
**AMMO CAPACITY:** HIGH **RELOAD TIME:** MID

### ELIMINATE BUILDINGS AND PLAYERS IN MOMENTS

Spraying down anyone who might dare to walk within a
few feet of you is the most useful aspect of the SMG.
However, one overlooked use of the weapon is to take
down buildings, which this little monster's improved
stats help out with. Even though it doesn't have amazing
structure damage on paper, the sheer rate of fire means
it still works wonders, and you may even land a few shots
before the occupant can start to rebuild.

# RARE
## SUBMACHINE GUN

**DAMAGE:** LOW **FIRE RATE:** HIGH
**AMMO CAPACITY:** HIGH **RELOAD TIME:** MID

### A RIDICULOUS DPS MACHINE

In reality, the Rare SMG isn't that much of an upgrade over the Common version in most situations. However, when it comes to weapons to use up close, there are few better options, especially if you don't trust your ability to land Shotgun blasts. You'll almost always see someone running a Shotgun, but not that many carry a Submachine Gun into the late game, and it could be a solid choice.

# BURST SMG

## COMMON
### BURST SMG

**DAMAGE:** LOW **FIRE RATE:** HIGH
**AMMO CAPACITY:** MID **RELOAD TIME:** MID

### NEED HELP KEEPING YOUR FIRE RATE IN CHECK?

Rate of fire is the main selling point of the SMG family. So why would you want to limit that with a burst-fire variant? The answer is simple—the weapon becomes easier to control even if you panic, although you'll want to be on the lookout for the rarer versions as they hit a little harder.

# UNCOMMON
## BURST SMG

**DAMAGE:** LOW **FIRE RATE:** HIGH
**AMMO CAPACITY:** MID **RELOAD TIME:** MID

### TWO TAPS, ONE DOWN

Although the damage boost this version gets over the basic one is low, it's significant in that it allows the Burst SMG to down any opponent in two bursts to the body where all shots connect. Given that you can get those two bursts off in the space of a second, this is an amazing option for anyone who struggles to land close-range headshots.

## TIP
SMGs use up their bullets very quickly due to their rapid-fire nature. Use controlled bursts to save ammo.

# RARE
## BURST SMG

**DAMAGE:** LOW **FIRE RATE:** HIGH
**AMMO CAPACITY:** MID **RELOAD TIME:** MID

### MASTER THE KICK TO MASTER THE SHORT GAME

It can be hard to land headshots consistently with fast-firing weapons, which is where burst-fire guns come in handy. With time, you can learn exactly how the gun kicks each time you pull the trigger and start to compensate for it accordingly. If you can get all four shots of a single burst to connect with the head, only a fully shielded opponent is going to remain standing afterward.

# SUPPRESSED SUBMACHINE GUN

## COMMON
## SUPPRESSED SUBMACHINE GUN

**DAMAGE:** LOW **FIRE RATE:** HIGH
**AMMO CAPACITY:** HIGH **RELOAD TIME:** LOW

### A QUIET LITTLE HALFWAY HOUSE

The Suppressed Submachine Gun is a strange one in the world of SMGs. It has the highest base damage of an SMG, but also the lowest fire rate, almost putting it in between SMGs and rifles in terms of stats. It also has the benefit of being near-silent, letting you get the drop on opponents.

# UNCOMMON
## SUPPRESSED SUBMACHINE GUN

**DAMAGE:** LOW **FIRE RATE:** HIGH
**AMMO CAPACITY:** HIGH **RELOAD TIME:** LOW

### THIS IS SILENT. LASERS ARE SILENT. COINCIDENCE?

Most SMGs are solid options for bringing down buildings, but the Suppressed SMG has the advantage of being able to do it stealthily. Knowing where shots are coming from is vitally important if your structure is under siege. But if silenced shots are raining in, it becomes super difficult to tell where they come from and that's why it's good to have this weapon on your side.

**FACT**
The Suppressed SMG has among the best accuracy stat of any automatic weapon in Fortnite.

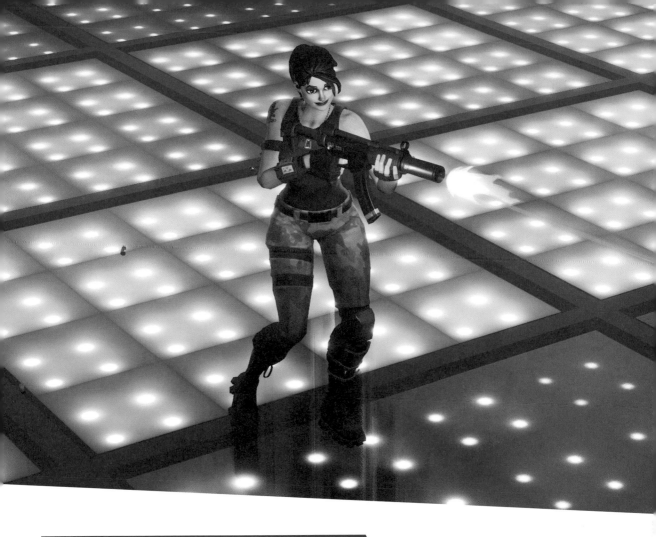

# RARE
## SUPPRESSED SUBMACHINE GUN

**DAMAGE:** LOW **FIRE RATE:** HIGH
**AMMO CAPACITY:** HIGH **RELOAD TIME:** LOW

### STEALTHIER THAN A NINJA IN THE NIGHT

When it comes to SMGs, the damage increase for
rarity isn't all that significant, but here the higher
headshot damage is a big factor. Anyone who isn't at
maximum health and shields will most likely go down in
four or fewer headshots, which can easily be delivered
by skilled players before you figure out where the
shots are coming from.

# TACTICAL SUBMACHINE GUN

## UNCOMMON
### TACTICAL SUBMACHINE GUN

**DAMAGE:** LOW **FIRE RATE:** HIGH
**AMMO CAPACITY:** HIGH **RELOAD TIME:** MID

### A MASTER CLASS IN STRATEGY

At close range, this little beauty can outclass almost any other weapon. Its high rate of fire and DPS—currently the highest in Fortnite—make it truly fearsome to come up against. It's also very adept at bringing down structures in a hail of bullets.

# RARE
## TACTICAL SUBMACHINE GUN

**DAMAGE:** LOW **FIRE RATE:** HIGH
**AMMO CAPACITY:** HIGH **RELOAD TIMES:** MID

### EXCELLENT UP CLOSE

It may not have the one-shot, one-elimination potential of the Pump Shotgun, but make no mistake, the Rare Tactical SMG is an absolute monster in close quarters. Try circle-strafing targets to land damage while avoiding taking hits yourself.

"[THE TACTICAL SMG] CAN COMPETE WITH THE SHOTGUNS AND HONESTLY COULD BE EVEN BETTER."
**ALI-A**

# EPIC
## TACTICAL SUBMACHINE GUN

**DAMAGE:** LOW **FIRE RATE:** HIGH
**AMMO CAPACITY:** HIGH **RELOAD TIME:** LOW

### EVENTUALLY, ALL TACTICS ARE FIGURED OUT

In its final form, the only real downside to the Epic Tactical SMG was the short range that all SMGs have. Its damage per second is unreal, the accuracy at close range is good enough to allow you to spray and control it easily, and a surprisingly quick reload time for a weapon with a large bullet capacity means even messing up leaves you with a chance to get back into the fight.

# COMPACT SMG

## FACT
Although very good for bringing down buildings, the Compact SMG is actually very slightly slower than the Suppressed SMG.

## EPIC
### COMPACT SMG

**DAMAGE:** LOW **FIRE RATE:** HIGH
**AMMO CAPACITY:** HIGH **RELOAD TIME:** MID

**BRINGS BUILDINGS DOWN IN SECONDS**

With a high rate of fire and large ammo capacity, this little beauty makes short work of foes and structures alike. With no penalties for continuous fire, it works especially well while you're on the move. It may have a three-second reload time—enough time for an enemy to take a Shield Potion—but this is one of the most capable weapons in the game.

# LEGENDARY
## COMPACT SMG

**DAMAGE:** LOW **FIRE RATE:** HIGH
**AMMO CAPACITY:** HIGH **RELOAD TIME:** MID

### SIZE ISN'T EVERYTHING, AND THIS LITTLE MONSTER PROVES IT!

As the name suggests, this is a small weapon, but it's one with massive ammo capacity and solid damage. You really can just spray bullets at your opponent, or any structure, until they go down and you don't have to worry too much about the reload speed, which is comparatively slow. It loses accuracy at medium range and beyond, but this was designed for getting up close and personal and taking the enemy out before they know what's hit them.

# KNOWLEDGE IS POWER!

## ALWAYS OUTNUMBERED, NEVER OUTGUNNED

The chaos of the Large Team Modes means that individual weapon choices aren't as important as they are in clutch 1v1 situations. Just make sure you've got something reliable, and get into a position where you can make it sing—there's no sense in sitting at the back of the pack with a Shotgun, after all!

# FIRE IN THE HOLE!

## ITEMS TO HELP YOU WIN BIG

Consumable items in Fortnite come in all shapes and sizes, from explosives that can deal high damage to unique pickups. As with weapons, your limited inventory space means it's important to know what you're picking up, so we've prepared a rundown of all the key (and some no longer available) items in the game to help you loot more efficiently. The right item can catch an opponent off guard or be just what you need to quickly punch a hole in their defenses.

## APPLES

**TYPE: HEALING**

This all-natural healing item may only restore a small amount of HP, but its existence makes escaping into forests or orchards a valid strategy. Pick some fruit to top yourself up without eating into your healing supplies, since apples are consumed on interaction.

## BALLOONS

**TYPE: MOBILITY**

These inflatables are more useful than you might expect. You can attach up to three to yourself at a time. The first two increase jump height and slow fall speed, and the third makes you float up. Careful, though: If they get popped, you'll plummet to the ground and take damage.

## BANANAS

**TYPE: HEALING**

Fortnite's ever-expanding list of biomes has made it so that finding apples everywhere is no longer realistic. In tropical areas, expect to find bananas instead, which serve exactly the same function of restoring a little health, but in a new and decidedly bendier package.

## BANDAGES

**TYPE: HEALING**

One of the more common healing items, bandages offer a small heal when used and come in stacks of five. They can only do so much, though—bandages can't heal you past 75HP, so you'll need to find something a little more potent to get back to full health.

# BOOGIE BOMB

**TYPE:** UTILITY

Make your opponents surrender to the beat with these groovy grenades! They don't deal direct damage but anyone caught in the blast is forced to dance for five seconds (or until damage is taken), making them perfect for taking a player or group out of the action.

# BOOM BOX

**TYPE:** UTILITY

More weaponized music—only this doesn't affect players. Its powerful shockwaves deal large damage to nearby structures, but only at short range. While it could wreak havoc on things like towers, it was made obsolete by the more versatile Bottle Rockets in Season 7.

# BOTTLE ROCKETS

**TYPE:** DAMAGE/UTILITY

Players caught in the blasts from these mini missiles take a small amount of damage, but they're more effective on structures. Set them off then get moving, as they also serve as their own form of suppressing fire to cover your approach or retreat.

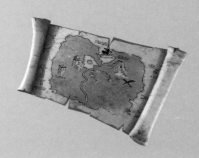

# BURIED TREASURE

**TYPE:** UTILITY

Tied into Season 8's pirate theme, this incredible item was perfect for getting a whole squad outfitted instantly. By following the trail that appeared when it was held, treasure hunters would eventually find a stash of top-end weapons and items all for themselves.

# BUSH

**TYPE: UTILITY**

We've all hidden away in a bush at some point, but this rare pickup brings the foliage to you for once! With this, you can don a cunning disguise that lets you blend in with any grassy area, although bear in mind that your cover will be blown if you're wearing it anywhere shrubs shouldn't be!

# CAKE SLICE

**TYPE: HEALING**

Cakes could be found around the map during the celebration period, with each slice restoring a small amount of health and shields. Sadly, Fortnite's map is currently devoid of cake, but who knows what future birthday celebrations might bring?

# CHILLER GRENADE

**TYPE: UTILITY**

Don't let that smiley face fool you, this grenade still does damage. Throw it, and any enemies within the blast radius are knocked back and hit with the effects of a Chiller trap for 7 seconds, causing them to skid around out of control. It's great for causing moments of disruption.

# CHUG JUG

**TYPE: HEALING**

The ultimate healing item. This drink restores health and shields to their maximum values, but it takes a whopping 15 seconds to down the lot, so make sure you're safe before you take your first sip. Either build yourself cover or have allies distract any nearby opponents.

# CHUG SPLASH

**TYPE: HEALING**

If you enjoy playing a healing role, this useful product on the curative soft drink market will be your go-to item. Unlike the other drinks, this one is used by throwing it at a location, where the explosion of liquid will restore a small amount of health or shields to anyone nearby.

# CLINGER

**TYPE: DAMAGE**

This improvised sticky grenade is a potent tool in the right hands. While the suction cap makes it look like it is designed to stick to vertical surfaces (where it can easily blow holes in walls), it also functions just as well when attaching to other players!

# COCONUTS

**TYPE: HEALING**

Nature's answer to Slurp Juice, in that coconuts will restore a small amount of health, or give you some shield power if your health is already full. As with other fruit and vegetables in Fortnite, these are consumed instantly upon pickup rather than being sent to your inventory.

# DYNAMITE

**TYPE: DAMAGE**

If it's a big boom you want, then you're in the right place. This crude explosive deals a lot of damage over a large radius, shredding players and structures alike. Its long fuse gives enemies a fair bit of time to get away. But that can be just as good for flushing them out of an area.

# GLIDER

**TYPE:** MOBILITY

If you want to use your Glider after the initial descent, you'll need to grab a stack of these consumables. The Glider is a fantastic way to cover distance, so get some height and soar away from the incoming Storm Circle. That gives you time to prepare before everyone else gets near.

# GRAPPLER

**TYPE:** MOBILITY

Mobility can be a lifesaver in Fortnite, and there are few better emergency exit options than this. It's a portable grappling hook that can allow you to yank yourself out of a fight as a last resort, or to get set up on high ground before an opponent can react to your movement.

# GRENADE

**TYPE:** DAMAGE

This classic is more than capable of eliminating unshielded opponents caught in its blast radius. Again, you can use this to flush players out of cover and into the open—make them choose between getting blown up or running into the sights of your waiting team.

# IMPULSE GRENADE

**TYPE:** UTILITY

This doesn't do direct damage, but knocking back anything in the blast zone can have some creative and powerful uses. A shotgun rusher isn't going to enjoy being bumped out of their effective range while you pick them off, for instance.

# JETPACK

**TYPE:** MOBILITY

If balloons are too crude a method of travel for you, this backpack will likely do the trick. Its engines overheat easily, so it's not well suited to covering long distances or great heights, but the extra mobility it offers is still a huge help. Use it in short, controlled bursts.

# JEWEL

**TYPE:** UTILITY

The shiny win condition for the Getaway Limited Time Mode. While this large llama-shaped gemstone doesn't have any practical use, players in the Getaway mode need to be the first to escape with one of these priceless crystals in order to win the game for their team.

# MEDKIT

**TYPE:** HEALING

Your go-to source of major heals in most combat situations. This medical supply kit can fully restore health, but takes 10 seconds to fully apply—while that might not sound like too long, it can feel like an eternity when you know there are enemies just around the corner.

# MUSHROOM

**TYPE:** HEALING

Foraging for wild mushrooms can give your shields a bit of a boost, and each one you chomp adds five points' worth of protection. While that's not much, it's still great for fixing minor dents in your defenses and saving Shield Potions for when you need them more.

# PEPPER

**TYPE: HEALING/MOBILITY**

An all-natural upgrade to the apple for anyone looking to spice up their play. In addition to giving a small heal on consumption, this fiery treat also increases your movement speed by 20% for a short time, letting you cover ground more quickly.

# PORT-A-FORT

**TYPE: UTILITY**

This rare item is the first instant build grenade in Fortnite. It creates a small tower where it lands, with tires to bounce you up to a battlement at the top that's ideal for sniper fire. Be warned though, it's vulnerable to taking enemy fire during deployment.

# PORT-A-FORTRESS

**TYPE: UTILITY**

If you thought the Port-A-Fort was a cheap way to get a defensive leg up, get a load of this! Instead of a tower, this rare grenade spawns an entire castle that can easily protect a whole team with room to spare.

# PRESENTS

**TYPE: UTILITY**

This festive care package has a good chance to spawn Legendary weapons upon use, making it a great way to gear up should you happen to find one. Naturally, they're seasonal exclusives and don't tend to stick around for long, but they are fun while they last.

## REMOTE EXPLOSIVES

**TYPE: DAMAGE**

Who needs fuses and timers when you can make things go boom whenever you like? These potent tools can be used to set off near-instant explosions or deployed as traps to fortify a position.

## RIFT-TO-GO

**TYPE: MOBILITY**

What better way to take to the skies than by tearing a hole in space and time? It's an amazing way to make a quick escape from trouble, although bear in mind that the rift entrance you create remains in place for several seconds after use, allowing friends and foes to follow you through.

## SHADOW BOMB

**TYPE: UTILITY/MOBILITY**

A versatile item with two distinct benefits. The first is that it turns you into a shadowy form for a brief time, making you much harder to see. The second is greatly enhanced movement, allowing double-jumps and wall jumps to help you get to otherwise unreachable places.

## SHADOW STONES

**TYPE: MOBILITY**

Part of Season 6's theme of corruption, these gems made getting around the map a breeze. They transform players into phantom-like versions of themselves with increased mobility and semi-invisibility, as well as the ability to phase through objects, although weapons can't be used.

## SHIELD POTION

**TYPE:** HEALING

Each of these defense-boosting potions can restore up to 50 points to your shields, and there's no cooldown so you're free to glug through two in a row to max out. Since there's a lesser version of this item, it's a good idea to only use big ones when they can deliver full potency.

## SHOCKWAVE GRENADE

**TYPE:** UTILITY

Effectively an upgraded version of the Impulse Grenade, this has the same effect of knocking back anyone or anything caught in the blast radius, although affected players will take no fall damage.

## SLURP JUICE

**TYPE:** HEALING

Unlike many curative items, using a jar of Slurp Juice is extremely quick. Its effects, however, are not, and rather than a burst of healing, this drink provides 2HP per second for around 40 seconds. It can also overheal to restore shields once your HP is full.

## SMALL SHIELD POTION

**TYPE:** HEALING

These minor shield heals might seem like a waste of inventory space, but the solution is simply to not carry them around. Grab them where you find them, use what you need, then dump the rest.

# SMOKE GRENADE

**TYPE:** UTILITY

Toss one of these grenades into an area and laugh with evil glee as your foes are surrounded by a cloud of vision-impairing smoke. It doesn't cause damage, but it's useful for moments where you want to sow a little confusion and get the jump on your opponents.

# SNEAKY SNOWMAN

**TYPE:** UTILITY

Pretending to be a bush is cool, but pretending to be a snowman is cooler. This wintry special allows you to deploy several small snowmen, which can be used as cover or distractions.

# STINK BOMB

**TYPE:** DAMAGE

Gross out opponents with this gas grenade. This is best suited to dealing with armored enemies, since it deals 5 damage every half second, chewing straight through health without worrying about shields. Most players will be quick to leave the cloud as soon as it appears.

# STORM FLIP

**TYPE:** DAMAGE/UTILITY

Using the Storm to eliminate enemies has always been a good strategy, and this item makes it even more practical. When thrown, a Storm bubble grows from the blast, making this an amazing area denial tool. Conversely, using it within the Storm creates a small pocket of safety.

# ACCURACY IS EVERYTHING

## WHO NEEDS RAPID FIRE WHEN YOU'VE GOT THE POWER OF A PRECISION WEAPON IN YOUR HANDS?

Fortnite has a lot of weapons to choose from, and each suits a certain style of play. But for many players, nothing compares to the power of a precision gun. The hitboxes and accuracy of these weapons are quite forgiving compared to other games, but you do need to learn how to effectively utilize them. You'll also need to pick the right situation—only experienced players risk using a sniper rifle in the middle of a hectic gunfight!

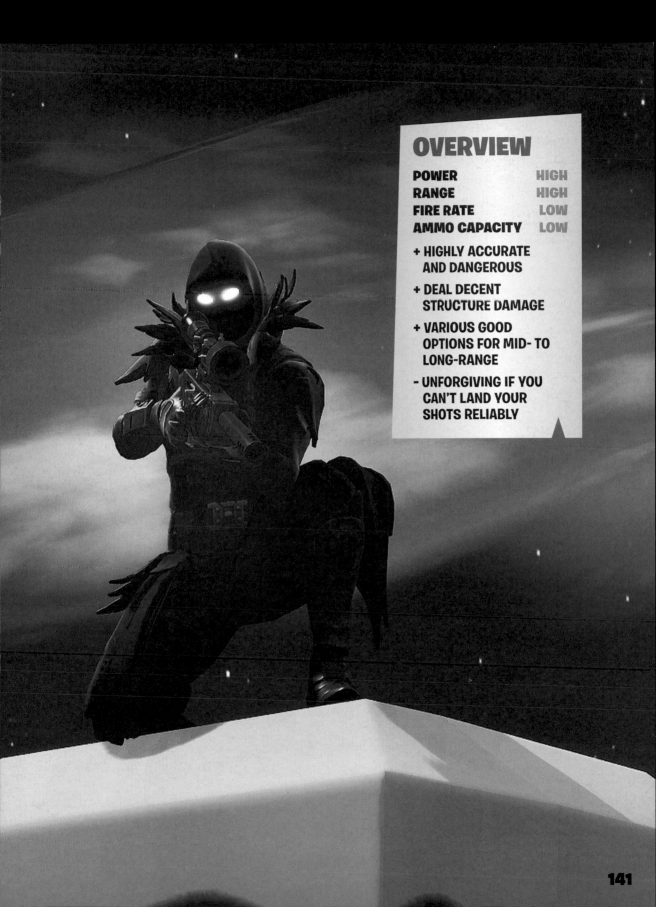

## OVERVIEW

| | |
|---|---|
| POWER | HIGH |
| RANGE | HIGH |
| FIRE RATE | LOW |
| AMMO CAPACITY | LOW |

+ HIGHLY ACCURATE AND DANGEROUS

+ DEAL DECENT STRUCTURE DAMAGE

+ VARIOUS GOOD OPTIONS FOR MID- TO LONG-RANGE

- UNFORGIVING IF YOU CAN'T LAND YOUR SHOTS RELIABLY

# CROSSBOW

## EPIC
### CUPID'S CROSSBOW

**DAMAGE:** HIGH **FIRE RATE:** LOW
**AMMO CAPACITY:** LOW **RELOAD TIME:** MID

**SHOW OTHER PLAYERS WHO'S
BOSS WITH A FEW BOLTS!**

The crossbow might not be the most popular weapon,
but it can be a game-changer. With five shots per
magazine, it's much more forgiving than things like the
Heavy and Bolt-Action Sniper Rifles.

# HUNTING RIFLE

## HUNTING RIFLE

**DAMAGE:** HIGH **FIRE RATE:** LOW
**AMMO CAPACITY:** LOW **RELOAD TIME:** LOW

### THE GENTLEMAN'S SNIPER RIFLE

The Hunting Rifle is one of Fortnite's hidden gems. It may seem like a middling combination of a sniper rifle and an assault rifle, but it's a weapon that has far more potential. Even with its noticeable bullet drop at long distances, it's incredibly versatile. It doesn't have a scope, but it offers increased zoom compared to other non-scoped weapon variants.

**TIP**
Hunting Rifles do 2.5x damage on critical hits, so a single headshot is enough to down any player.

# RARE
## HUNTING RIFLE

**DAMAGE:** HIGH **FIRE RATE:** LOW
**AMMO CAPACITY:** LOW **RELOAD TIME:** LOW

### THE MIDRANGE MONSTER OF FORTNITE

While it shares the same fire rate as its Uncommon iteration, the Rare Hunting Rifle has enhanced stats that make it a powerful gun. Especially useful in the endgame of a match, its midrange and long-range capacity makes it really useful when the eye of the Storm is shrinking around you. It also has a relatively quick reload time and a respectable damage output.

## TIP
Miss the Hunting Rifle? Give the Infantry Rifle a try—it's more forgiving and easier to use.

## EPIC
### HEAVY SNIPER RIFLE

**DAMAGE:** HIGH **FIRE RATE:** LOW
**AMMO CAPACITY:** LOW **RELOAD TIME:** HIGH

**A BEEFY LONG-RANGE STAPLE**

The Epic variant of the Heavy Sniper Rifle is the kind of gun you're always hoping to find in a chest or loot from a fallen player. Why? Well, despite its relatively slow reload time, this iteration still packs an enormous punch compared to every other precision weapon in the game.

# LEGENDARY
## HEAVY SNIPER RIFLE

**DAMAGE:** HIGH **FIRE RATE:** LOW
**AMMO CAPACITY:** LOW **RELOAD TIME:** HIGH

### UNLEASH THE LONG-RANGED BEAST

The Heavy Sniper Rifle packs the biggest damage and the longest range in the game. This is the preferred choice for many experienced snipers thanks to its great damage, which is also useful against structures. It can be a little slow to aim, but with a built-in muzzle brake and a powerful scope, this can be a game-changer.

## TIP
The Heavy Sniper Rifle is one of the few weapons in Fortnite with almost no bullet drop at long distances. Very useful.

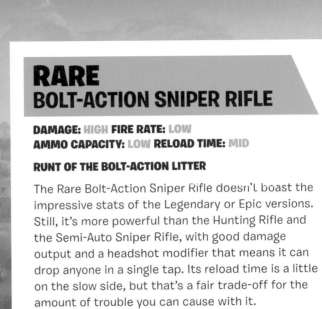

# RARE
## BOLT-ACTION SNIPER RIFLE

**DAMAGE:** HIGH **FIRE RATE:** LOW
**AMMO CAPACITY:** LOW **RELOAD TIME:** MID

### RUNT OF THE BOLT-ACTION LITTER

The Rare Bolt-Action Sniper Rifle doesn't boast the impressive stats of the Legendary or Epic versions. Still, it's more powerful than the Hunting Rifle and the Semi-Auto Sniper Rifle, with good damage output and a headshot modifier that means it can drop anyone in a single tap. Its reload time is a little on the slow side, but that's a fair trade-off for the amount of trouble you can cause with it.

# EPIC
## BOLT-ACTION SNIPER RIFLE

**DAMAGE:** HIGH **FIRE RATE:** LOW
**AMMO CAPACITY:** LOW **RELOAD TIME:** MID

### A RANGED GUN YOU CAN'T WAIT TO FIND

The Epic Bolt-Action Sniper Rifle is the kind of gun you simply can't wait to get your hands on. This is especially true when you're approaching the endgame of a match and everyone is building fortifications. With great damage output, this powerful rifle can one-shot other players, so long as you can line up your angles right.

# LEGENDARY
## BOLT-ACTION SNIPER RIFLE

**DAMAGE:** HIGH **FIRE RATE:** LOW
**AMMO CAPACITY:** LOW **RELOAD TIME:** MID

### UNLEASHING HELL FROM AFAR

The Bolt-Action Sniper Rifle is one of the most powerful precision weapons in Fortnite. At Legendary rarity, the Bolt-Action Sniper Rifle is even more formidable, with headshot damage values that are pure overkill—this thing is able to one-tap any player, regardless of health and shields. The only caveat is its slow reload speed.

## TIP
If you're carrying two Bolt-Action Sniper Rifles you can aim, fire, switch rifles, and fire again.

## UNCOMMON
### SEMI-AUTO SNIPER RIFLE

**DAMAGE:** HIGH **FIRE RATE:** LOW
**AMMO CAPACITY:** MID **RELOAD TIME:** MID

**MORE BULLETS MEANS MORE DAMAGE**

Not as powerful as the Hunting Rifle, but it does however boast a larger magazine. This makes it far more forgiving to less experienced players. Those extra bullets enable you to suppress enemy squads from afar, but unless you land headshots, one of those bullets doesn't do a huge amount of damage to a shield or to the body.

## TIP
While it's not quite as powerful as some rifles, its 10-round capacity makes it good for laying down suppressing fire.

# RARE
## SEMI-AUTO SNIPER RIFLE

**DAMAGE:** HIGH **FIRE RATE:** LOW
**AMMO CAPACITY:** MID **RELOAD TIME:** MID

### A RELIABLE RANGED WEAPON

In its highest rarity, the Semi-Auto Sniper Rifle is a powerful weapon. The Rare version packs some modest damage output and while it won't always be able to one-shot an enemy, the larger magazine size ensured that you usually have enough ammo in reserve. With higher damage potential than its Uncommon iteration, it's a decent little rifle.

## TIP
Quickly scoping before firing will usually lead to more precise hits with sniper rifles. It won't guarantee a hit, but it'll up your chances.

# SUPPRESSED SNIPER RIFLE

## EPIC
### SUPPRESSED SNIPER RIFLE

**DAMAGE:** HIGH **FIRE RATE:** LOW
**AMMO CAPACITY:** LOW **RELOAD TIME:** MID

#### ENJOY THE SILENCE

If you get frustrated when you're picked off by a sniper, this will be your worst nightmare. The ability to one-shot unshielded foes anywhere on the body is amazing, but the real benefit is that you can do it so much more quietly than with other rifles.

## TIP
Moving between vantage points when using a silenced weapon makes it even harder for opponents to track you.

# LEGENDARY
## SUPPRESSED SNIPER RIFLE

**DAMAGE:** HIGH **FIRE RATE:** LOW
**AMMO CAPACITY:** LOW **RELOAD TIME:** MID

### FROM OUT OF NOWHERE

There's not a vast improvement from the Epic to the Legendary version. The slightly faster reload speed might let you pop off a few more shots, but the damage boost isn't doing all that much—it's still going to take two shots to drop shielded enemies if you're not getting them in the head. Still, who doesn't enjoy finding a Legendary gun?

> **"IT LOOKS ABSOLUTELY AWESOME!"**
> **ALI-A**

## KNOWLEDGE IS POWER!

## A GOOD LANDING ZONE CAN MAKE A HUGE DIFFERENCE

Some areas are naturally richer in loot than others, although many of the best spots are also the most popular. It's up to you whether you'd rather gear up more slowly in the relative safety of the outskirts of the map, or brave a busy landing zone and hope that you find something good enough to carry you through the chaos that ensues!

# PERFECT PAIRINGS

## WHAT TO PACK ALONGSIDE YOUR FAVORITE WEAPONS

We all have our favorite guns in Fortnite. For some, nothing beats the thrill of getting up close and personal with a shotgun, while others prefer to pick off their prey from a safe distance with a high-powered sniper rifle. Whatever your weapon of choice, there will always come a time when you need something to back it up, and that will be different depending on what your own go-to gun happens to be. Sure, loot drops are somewhat random, but that doesn't mean you can't supplement your arsenal, be it by scooping up the Common weapons others leave behind or by stockpiling consumables or building materials to help your chosen play style. Don't be too snobbish about white or green weapons though—switching to one of these instead of reloading your one cherished shooter might just save you from a trip back to the main menu!

# ASSAULT RIFLES

## ALL-PURPOSE WEAPONS THAT CAN BE COUPLED WITH ANY OTHER GUN

Automatics are among the game's most versatile weapons. What you keep in reserve will depend on how you like to play and your preferred engagement range. For players who like to rush enemies, a shotgun can be a potent finishing blow. If you're fonder of the opposite end of the automatic rifle's effective range, you might consider the reverse—grab a sniper rifle, use that to pop shields from distance, then rush enemies with your automatic.

# SHOTGUNS

## YOU'VE GOT CLOSE QUARTERS COVERED, BUT YOU NEED SOMETHING WITH A BIT OF RANGE

The noble shotgun is only really effective when you're within a few feet of your opponent. As such, you're going to want to back it up with something that helps you close the gap. Most obvious would be to grab any rapid-firing weapon and use it to lay down suppressing fire. Accuracy and even landing hits don't really matter when the main goal is to force opponents into cover as you close the gap to get into shotgun range.

# PISTOLS/SMGS

### SMALL ARMS PACK A PUNCH, BUT PICK A BACKUP WITH STOPPING POWER

So you're something of a gunslinger? Then you already know how powerful these can be. Given the need for accuracy when using small arms, a logical secondary weapon would be a sniper rifle. However, if you love the pistol because it's the opposite style of play to sitting back and waiting for the perfect shot, keep an eye out for a ranged weapon that gels with your style rather than one that forces you down a different path. Try a rifle with a midrange scope, for instance.

# SNIPER RIFLES

### A MONSTER AT RANGE, BUT YOU'LL NEED SOMETHING FOR CLOSE ENCOUNTERS, TOO

For those who like to fight from a distance, there's nothing like a sniper rifle. But the sad truth is that not everyone will let you engage them at distance, so you still need to be prepared for close-quarters combat as well. If you're comfortable with hip-firing snipers then your best bet will be a shotgun or SMG, but if you're a hard-scoping sniper fan then you might be better suited to carrying an automatic for when you're in short- to midrange.

# EXPLOSIVES

## BLOWING THINGS UP ISN'T THE ANSWER TO EVERY PROBLEM... JUST MOST OF THEM

We get it, blowing things up is fun. But the main problem with explosive weapons and items is that they tend to be in short supply. As such, they're often best backed up with weapons with deeper ammo reserves. Hot-swapping between things that blow up walls and things that can make use of that brief vulnerability window is a great combo. Ping a grenade or two at an opponent's position, then switch to a rifle and make the best use you can of those few moments of panic.

# HERE COMES THE BOOM!

## FORGET HEADSHOTS AND STEALTH...THESE WEAPONS ARE ALL ABOUT CHAOS. GO IN LOUD AND COME OUT PROUD!

Weapons that end with a bang are hard to find in Fortnite. But if you do get one, you can become a one-person wrecking ball or a valuable member of a squad. Practically every pro player has spent time learning the quirks of explosives—from the speed of rockets to the bounce of grenades. Explosives do have a weakness—a hit can eliminate players or crumble defenses instantly, but if your shot misses, the reload time leaves you vulnerable. The noise is a problem too and will draw players to you or give away your position. Explosives are integral to your arsenal, though. Being able to deal massive amounts of damage will always be helpful and make opponents run for cover.

## OVERVIEW

| | |
|---|---|
| **POWER** | HIGH |
| **RANGE** | HIGH |
| **FIRE RATE** | LOW |
| **AMMO CAPACITY** | LOW |

+ CAN QUICKLY DESTROY BASES OR STRUCTURES

+ HANDY FOR CREATING LOUD DIVERSIONS

+ CAN SWIFTLY CHANGE THE TIDE OF A BATTLE

- LACK PRECISION AND ACCURACY

## RARE
### GRENADE LAUNCHER

**DAMAGE:** HIGH **FIRE RATE:** LOW
**AMMO CAPACITY:** MID **RELOAD TIME:** MID

#### ENTRY-LEVEL EXPLOSIVES

The lower rarity of this Grenade Launcher will mean it's easier to find, and ammo isn't too hard to come by, either. The chances of finding this weapon are high, so get used to seeing it and using it. It's not going to bring down huge structures, but it's great for creating a diversion.

## TIP

Many people know about rocket riding, but did you know you can ride grenades as well? Just be sure to hop off before it blows up!

## EPIC
### GRENADE LAUNCHER

**DAMAGE:** HIGH **FIRE RATE:** LOW
**AMMO CAPACITY:** MID
**RELOAD TIME:** MID

#### PURPLE PEOPLE SMASHER

With a quicker reload time and a boost in damage, this is the ideal middle road for a Grenade Launcher. It can make light work of wooden ramps and walls, while the extra damage makes precision less of a worry.

# LEGENDARY
## GRENADE LAUNCHER

**DAMAGE:** HIGH **FIRE RATE:** LOW
**AMMO CAPACITY:** MID **RELOAD TIME:** MID

### THE HOTTEST POTATO

Grenade Launchers will lay down more
DPS than a Rocket Launcher, but they lack
the precision. This variation will deal with
buildings, enemies, and vehicles brilliantly.
It's a great choice for firing explosives into an
area to blast a closely packed enemy squad.

# PROXIMITY GRENADE LAUNCHER

## EPIC
## PROXIMITY
## GRENADE LAUNCHER

**DAMAGE:** HIGH **FIRE RATE:** LOW
**AMMO CAPACITY:** LOW **RELOAD TIME:** MID

### CLOSE IS GOOD ENOUGH

The way grenades bounce around after being
fired can make the regular Grenade Launcher
tricky to use. But with this user-friendly upgrade,
grenades will detonate as soon as they get near
another player, and it's even easier to get them
there thanks to the weapon's useful scope.

## FACT
The Proximity Grenade
Launcher is the only
explosive weapon in
the game that boasts a
functional scope.

# LEGENDARY
## PROXIMITY
## GRENADE LAUNCHER

**DAMAGE:** HIGH **FIRE RATE:** LOW
**AMMO CAPACITY:** LOW **RELOAD TIME:** MID

### RAIN DOWN HAVOC FROM AFAR

Each grenade launched might do a fair bit less
damage than a standard Grenade Launcher round,
but it's much easier to connect with targets at
longer distances. A powerful launch also means
that rounds follow an extremely shallow trajectory.

# ROCKET LAUNCHER

## RARE
### ROCKET LAUNCHER

**DAMAGE:** HIGH **FIRE RATE:** LOW
**AMMO CAPACITY:** LOW **RELOAD TIME:** HIGH

### ROCKETING AND ROLLING

All Rocket Launchers are created equal when it comes to ammo capacity, holding only one rocket before needing to reload. The Rocket Launcher has a little more accuracy than the Grenade Launcher, and laying down cover fire can be done from a distance so you don't need to get close to those explosions. Ammo is quite plentiful, too, so fire off those rockets to your heart's content.

# EPIC
## ROCKET LAUNCHER

**DAMAGE:** HIGH **FIRE RATE:** LOW
**AMMO CAPACITY:** LOW **RELOAD TIME:** HIGH

### ROCKETING INTO THE CHARTS

A direct hit from an Epic Rocket Launcher is going
to make an unshielded foe disappear, plus it will cut
through wood like a knife through butter. Of course,
you can have lots of fun with a Rocket Launcher
away from eliminating opponents—players have
been known to rocket-ride using these weapons,
making travelling across the map a breeze.

# LEGENDARY
## ROCKET LAUNCHER

**DAMAGE:** HIGH **FIRE RATE:** LOW
**AMMO CAPACITY:** LOW **RELOAD TIME:** MID

### ROCKETING INTO OUR HEARTS

Damage that can shred stone walls or troublesome metal ramps, and a reload time quicker than a sniper rifle—this is the drop you want. If that wonderful orange glow surrounds a Rocket Launcher, you've got one of the best explosive weapons in the game. The damage per second cannot rival Grenade Launchers, but good aim can help you take out players or weaken squads, leaving them running for cover. If you've got time to search, there's no harm in looking for this truly Legendary weapon.

# QUAD LAUNCHER

## EPIC
### QUAD LAUNCHER

**DAMAGE:** HIGH **FIRE RATE:** LOW
**AMMO CAPACITY:** LOW **RELOAD TIME:** HIGH

### FOUR TIMES THE POWER?

It's easy to think that multiplying rockets would make for a bigger bang, but these weapons actually clock up less damage than regular Rocket Launchers. They also take almost twice as long to reload and chew through your ammo stash at a pace. So why use one? To scare everyone else, of course! If it's all you can find, it can still terrify an enemy or destroy their buildings.

## FACT
The missiles fired by the Quad Launcher drop fairly quickly, making this a great mortar-like tool for bombarding enemies who are behind cover.

# LEGENDARY
## QUAD LAUNCHER

**DAMAGE:** HIGH **FIRE RATE:** LOW
**AMMO CAPACITY:** LOW **RELOAD TIME:** HIGH

### FOUR TIMES THE FUN!

So, the rockets don't do as much damage, but Fortnite is
about having fun as well as winning. What's more fun than
four rockets speeding through the air to destroy a base
or structure? More about style over substance, the Quad
Launcher looks amazing, and you feel cool carrying one of these
around. It's probably at its best when used as your "swag"
weapon—the one you fall back on when you want to show off a
little bit or create a highlight clip to put online.

# GUIDED MISSILE

## EPIC
### GUIDED MISSILE

**DAMAGE:** HIGH **FIRE RATE:** LOW
**AMMO CAPACITY:** LOW **RELOAD TIME:** MID

### YOU CAN RUN, BUT YOU CAN'T HIDE

While its damage isn't the best, the fire rate and environmental damage of the Epic Guided Missile mean that players can annihilate buildings in no time at all. On top of that, these rockets are controlled by you, so even though they leave you vulnerable, with practice you can aim through windows or gaps and still reach your enemy. Skilled players have been known to ride rockets while they are being guided by an ally.

# LEGENDARY
## GUIDED MISSILE

**DAMAGE:** HIGH **FIRE RATE:** LOW
**AMMO CAPACITY:** LOW **RELOAD TIME:** MID

### TARGET LOCATED

Another reason why the Guided Missile became a favorite among players isn't its destructive capabilities or even the cool tricks, but the fact that it enables you to scope out an area from new angles. If you think someone is hiding in a building, you can do a flyby with a missile to confirm. If you want to see how many people are crouched behind a wall, missiles become surveillance drones, which can then be swung around in an arc to cause chaos from behind as you attack from the front.

## TIP

If you direct your missile back toward yourself and make a precisely timed jump, then it's possible to land on it and take a ride!

## KNOWLEDGE IS POWER!

## COME OUT SWINGING
## IF YOU NEED TO

Melee attacks might not be particularly powerful,
but they're fast and free. If an opponent is weak and
you're low on ammo, it's sometimes a good idea to
finish the job with your trusty Harvesting Tool—you'll
have plenty of time to reload once you're in the
clear, so always be aware of this option, as it might
just be the difference between life and elimination!

# TRAPPER'S DELIGHT

## CREATE YOUR OWN WEAPONS WITH THIS DEVIOUS SELECTION OF TOOLS

Fortnite's Battle Royale mode might have plenty of guns to find, load, and unleash, but they're not the only way to fight your fellow players. When used properly, traps can be some of the cleverest and most effective ways to take out multiple players at once. They can also be a way to buy time to heal yourself mid-fight, or be a means of changing the tide of battle in an instant.

0 | 100
100 | 100

MEMORY USED

10,524 | 100,000

# TRAPS: DECLASSIFIED

## DAMAGE TRAP

This is the classic trap and one of the most commonly found in Battle Royale. The Damage Trap causes 150 damage to anyone who steps on or in front of it. It's full of spikes, naturally.

## COZY CAMPFIRE

Things can get pretty heated in Fortnite. That's why it pays to have a Cozy Campfire to hand. Use it to slowly refill your health, preferably while you're behind some fortified cover.

## LAUNCH PAD

The Launch Pad is a pad that launches you into the air. It really is that simple. This trap doesn't cause damage, but it's ideal for making a quick escape or for reaching high ground quickly.

# JUMP PAD (DIRECTIONAL)

Later replaced by the far more versatile Launch Pad, this Jump Pad was designed to give you a lot more control over which direction you would launch when used.

# RETRACTABLE FLOOR SPIKES

One of the original traps in the game, the Retractable Floor Spikes trap is a reusable object that was Vaulted and replaced by the Damage Trap item.

# MOUNTED TURRET

This trap offers a mountable gun emplacement with infinite ammo. Be careful though—it's stationary and can overheat very easily.

# JUMP PAD (UP)

This was a variation of the directional Jump Pad that simply propelled you straight upwards. Like its bouncy relative, it was also replaced by the far simpler Launch Pad.

# BOUNCER

The Bouncer was a Rare trap that worked a lot like a Launch Pad, but without as much added height. Instead, the Bouncer platform would boost a jump while negating any fall damage.

# CHILLER

One of the only Common traps, the Chiller would reduce the amount of friction on your feet, enabling you to slide along the ground. It affected enemies and allies alike, making it also useful for tripping up foes.

# MAKE THE MOST OF TRAPS

## BUILD COVER OVER CAMPFIRES

Cozy Campfires can be used at any time, but unlike other health-restoring items in the game, you don't need to wait for an animation to finish. When the Storm Circle shrinks and you're in the endgame stage, build a short set of walls and a panel above to provide a small amount of cover, so you can heal and reload.

## AMBUSH WITH A DAMAGE TRAP ABOVE

Damage Traps are great if you can lure an opponent into walking on one, or coming close to one. Most players are wise to traps on the floor, so use one on the ceiling to catch them out. Whether in a house or a one-story fort, drop some decent items as bait, then you can just sit back and wait for the trap to be sprung.

## PLACE A LAUNCH PAD HIGH FOR THE MOST IMPACT

The Launch Pad doesn't produce a massive jump, although it can carry you very long distances if used along with your Glider. A good way to utilize it, especially if you are trying to reach another player, is to build your fort high and place the Launch Pad on top.

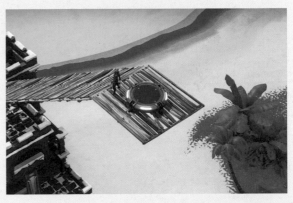

## PLACE A MOUNTED TURRET ON A SOLID SURFACE

It might seem like a good idea to build a moderately high fort and place a Mounted Turret on top. That way, you can pepper players below with unlimited ammo. That's true, but as soon as the panels below it are destroyed, the trap itself will break too, and you'll likely follow soon after. Aim to place Mounted Turrets on solid surfaces only.

# FAQS

## EVERYTHING YOU NEED TO KNOW ABOUT WEAPONS AND ITEMS IN FORTNITE

### WHAT'S THE BEST WEAPON IN FORTNITE?

With so many different play styles, controller configurations, locations, situational variables, and so on, the honest answer is that there isn't one weapon that can be called the "best." In the right hands, any weapon—even a Common Pistol—can wreck entire teams, so maybe you're asking the wrong question. Maybe the question should be, "Which weapon would suit me best?" That's one that only you can answer, by experimenting for yourself to find out.

### BUT HOW CAN I TRY OUT NEW WEAPONS WHEN THEY DROP RANDOMLY?

Playground Mode is the perfect place to mess around and try new things. All of the possible chest locations are active, materials are in abundance, and vending machines for special, powerful gear are also surprisingly common. All of this means that you can usually get your hands on anything you'll want within one sweep of the map, and even quicker if you bring a friend or two to help you hunt down what you're after. You'll need another player in the mode anyway if you want to test things like damage drop-off.

### WHAT ON EARTH IS DAMAGE DROP-OFF?

Every weapon has an effective range. If a target is within that distance, projectiles will deal their full amount of damage. As you get farther and farther outside of optimal range, however, damage gradually falls until

you reach the maximum range of the weapon, at which point the bullets will fail to reach the target at all. These ranges differ wildly between weapons, and learning them is important, whether that's to pull off shotgun eliminations from surprising distances, or simply to maximize your ammo efficiency and get the most out of each round.

## SOMETIMES WHEN I AIM AT AN OPPONENT'S HEAD, I GET REGULAR DAMAGE NUMBERS, NOT CRITICAL ONES. WHAT AM I DOING WRONG HERE?

Bullets don't fly in straight lines forever—the more distance they cover, the more they fall. When engaging at greater distances, you'll need to adjust your aim upward slightly to account for this. Similarly, you must also factor in bullet travel time. Fast as they are, they're not instant, so it's important to aim ahead of moving targets to land your shots. This is called "leading a target," and it's what separates great snipers from the rest of the pack.

## HOW CAN I CARRY MORE WEAPONS?

That's a nice easy one—you can't. Sorry. A big part of the game is having to make on-the-fly decisions about which gear you find is deserving of a valuable inventory slot, so you'll need to get used to leaving things behind. So long as you've got something for each major engagement range—close, medium, and long distance—and enough ammo for each, you should never need more than what Fortnite lets you carry.

# WHAT DOES DPS MEAN?

DPS stands for "Damage Per Second," and is a rough idea of how much hurt a gun can do, reached by multiplying its base damage by the amount of rounds it can fire per second. It doesn't take into account critical damage from headshots, so it can make some weapons seem worse than they actually are!

## IS A LEGENDARY WEAPON A ONE-WAY TICKET TO A VICTORY ROYALE?

Absolutely not. While top-tier weapons certainly have the highest damage output and the greatest amount of room for user error, even the best guns in the game do zero damage if you can't hit your target! Blaming weapon drops on losses is common, but not helpful—if you want to improve as a player, understanding that you can still come out on top even with inferior gear to an opponent is a crucial thing to remember. Instead of complaining that you're not finding rarer things, try to dissect each defeat to work out how you could have played better with the tools you actually had.

## WHEN WILL [MY FAVORITE WEAPON TYPE] BE ADDED TO THE GAME?

Who knows? Fortnite is a game that grows and evolves on a regular basis, and new weapons and

items are introduced with minimal warning all the time. Assuming what you want isn't too crazy, there's a good chance you'll get to play around with something similar at some point, even if only briefly as part of a Limited Time Mode.

## WHERE SHOULD I DROP IN?

Well, that depends on what kind of experience you're looking for, and how you like to play the game in general. Leaping at the first opportunity and heading for the nearest named location is a guaranteed way to get in a quick and hectic encounter with other players, although you'll need a lot of skill and probably more than a little luck to make it out of there in one piece. Conversely, biding your time and using your Glider to reach somewhere far from the Battle Bus's path

will usually give you more time to gear up and play the long game, at the risk of having further to go when the Storm shrinks. Try out all approaches and see what works out best for you.

## WHAT ARE HOT SPOTS?

If you see a location's name in yellow on the map, that means it's a Hot Spot. A different location (sometimes more than one) is chosen each game, and these areas offer more rare gear than other places thanks to the

Loot Carriers that spawn there. Shooting these down can be risky since gunfire is likely to attract other players (as is the allure of better loot), but the rewards are often worth the risk. Cunning players may even want to camp out these locations and use the carriers as bait, just like you can do with Supply Drops.

## HOW MUCH AMMO SHOULD I CARRY?

As much as possible! Since ammunition doesn't use up any inventory slots, there's no harm in grabbing as much as you find, even if you don't have a weapon that can use it—you never know what you might find later. In group play it pays to be more methodical in order to ensure that everyone on the team has ammo for their weapons. Don't hog all the heavy rounds if your buddy is the only one with a sniper rifle!

# DO WEAPONS AFFECT MOVEMENT SPEED?

This is something we've seen a lot of chatter about, but no—whether you're only carrying your starting Harvesting Tool or you're lugging a great big Minigun or Rocket Launcher around, your mobility is completely unaffected. Load up on heavy weapons to your heart's content, safe in the knowledge that you've got as much chance of escaping the Storm as everyone else!

First published in the UK in 2019 by WILDFIRE an imprint of HEADLINE PUBLISHING GROUP

Cataloguing in Publication Data is available from the British Library

Hardback 978 14722 6530 2

Design by Future plc.

Edited by Luke Albiges

All images © Epic Games, Inc.

Printed and bound in Italy by L.E.G.O. S.p.A.

**HEADLINE PUBLISHING GROUP**

An Hachette UK Company
Carmelite House, 50 Victoria Embankment
London, EC4 0DZ
www.headline.co.uk www.hachette.co.uk

Little, Brown and Company
Hachette Book Group
1290 Avenue of the Americas, New York, NY 10104
Visit us at hbgusa.com/fortnite

www.epicgames.com

**First Edition: October 2019**

First U.S. Edition: December 2019

Little, Brown and Company is a division of Hachette Book Group, Inc.

The Little, Brown name and logo are trademarks of Hachette Book Group, Inc.

The publisher is not responsible for websites (or their content) that are not owned by the publisher.

ISBNs: 978-0-316-53046-0 (paper over board), 978-0-316-53047-7 (ebook), 978-0-316-42481-3 (ebook), 978-0-316-42474-5 (ebook)

U.S. edition printed in United States of America

All images © Epic Games, Inc.

WAL

UK Hardback: 10 9 8 7 6 5 4 3 2 1
U.S. Paper Over Board: 10 9 8 7 6 5 4 3 2 1